The Africa Story:

One Musician's Perilous Foray into the World's Most Dangerous Jungle after the World's Most Precious Stones

MARK CHRISTIAN
& TROY CHRISTIAN

Troy, Tyler, and Mark Christian would like to dedicate this work to our new-found family member Michael Whitsitt

This isn't based on a true story -- it is a true story

PROLOGUE

My name is Mark Edward Christian, I was born in a hospital called Bella Vista which is near a town named Mayaguez which is on the island of Puerto Rico. My mother was a local and a member of a large family that bore the surname of Hernandez, My father hailed from Rhode Island but was raised in Norwalk,Connecticut. He had joined the Marines and was stationed in Arecibo, Puerto Rico where he and my mother met.

My earliest memories are of living in Norwalk with my mother, father, and older brother Daryl. I have a younger brother as well and his name is Christopher, I am 4 years and two months older than he is, and Daryl is two years older than I. From the very beginning there was turmoil in my parents lives and their union was short lived, I remember being ferried between Norwalk and Puerto Rico as they fought a lot and my mother would return home with us in tow. Memories of my dad are few but there are a few, mostly traumatic ones, contrasted with a moment or two of kindness towards me.

My parents had divorced by the time I was six years old and we spent a couple of years with my mother's family in Puerto Rico in that town of Mayaguez.

When I was eight years old my mother, who had moved to Florida with my brother Daryl, had her family ship me to her. My mother didn't speak English all that well at the time and obtaining work without any special degrees to her name was very hard. She had been very brave to try but soon found she needed help. She had always been very religious and a devout catholic and she turned to the catholic church for help. So the summer I was to turn 9 I found myself in the office of a man named Mr. Bennett. Mr Bennett was kind I suppose, he explained to me that I was being temporarily made a ward of the state in order for the church to be able to help my mother by placing us in what they termed a home. The "home" was an orphanage located in Tampa, Florida and known as The Christ Child Center. It shared a very large property with a school named St Lawrence, the school still stands today. The home is long gone.

My brother Christopher was primarily raised by my mother's sisters and we did not spend too much time together as children.

I have always considered myself to be kind of lucky within my unlucky circumstances. My older brother and I were raised in what we termed boarding schools, and my second home actually was a boarding school by the name of Mary Help of Christians which was also located in Tampa.

I remember becoming very independent rather quickly. My very first night at the orphanage I had to find a place in the pecking order of the all boys side of the home I was placed in. The alpha male at the time was a young blond headed boy maybe 2 or 3 years older than me, his name was Perry Gagnon. So in the middle of the boys side living room and under the watchful eye of a German nun by the name of Sister Okra we had a fist fight, as soon as it became apparent to me that the nun had no intention of interfering I discovered the great power of my temper. We were both pretty bloody, nose, lips, but I had already decided I would not yield to the older boy. I think I wore him down though, cause in order to save face Perry suggested we finish the fight in private, this is so funny now, the kids that were present about ten others, booed and jeered, but I didn't really know how much more I could take of this face punching stuff, so I accepted, once in there Perry turned out to be an okay kid, he said he had to keep his position as leader of our little pack of orphans, let him declare victory and I could be his friend. I thought I had proved my point and I agreed. Our pajamas were torn and bloody, buttons missing off the old style pajama tops. We shook hands and exited the small utility closet. I could tell by the look on Sister Okra's face that she thought she had done the right thing or maybe it was a bit of respect for me, I don't know. She never said a word about it.

Before we were sent off to the neighboring school everyday, we were each given a bag lunch and two dimes for a milk. I guess I was a big momma's boy and I worried a lot about my mother and how she might be. I had her phone number memorized and almost every night I would sneak out of the fire exit at the end of the boys side hallway, I would leave it propped open and I would walk barefoot across the school property and about a quarter mile to a gas station that was there, I would use those dimes to call my mother's number on the pay phone, If she answered I would hang up and always feeling much happier I would return to school, if I got no answer I would wait there by the payphone to try again, I'm not sure how long I would wait, but it felt long. Those kids became my family for the next five years. After CCC came the Mary Help of Christians years but I was out of there by the time I was 16 and it was on, imagine a dog seeing an ocean for the first time, that's how the freedom of not being in a school felt to me. And I tried to take full advantage of it. I thought everybody was this wild. I had to learn the hard way about alcohol and drugs and there was a dark period, but I somehow conquered that. And until the day my first known to me son was born I did what I wanted to do which was to be in a band and play music. The story you are about to read takes place a few years after becoming sober for the first time since I was 16.

CHAPTER 1

Two years of sobriety later, I was a different person. I had completely reforged my attitude in life and had quadrupled my abilities musically. I had found my own voice, and I was done with doing covers. I was in Miami on a day graced by a rare crispness—the sun was above me and my twenties behind me; I had just turned thirty years old. I was living in a brand new apartment in Kendall with a few sticks of furniture, stealing cable. There was a lot of burning the candle at both ends back then, and I would normally get home anywhere between midnight and 2 am and then get up at 7 to go to work. But I felt great; I was happy and very excited. Since getting sober, the possibilities were starting to seem endless. For the first time in my life, I was becoming an optimist.

So there I was, watching the news one evening, when I saw breaking news that Nelson Mandela had been released from prison. I had the TV on mute, as I strummed the guitar and wrote lyrics. My eyes kept going to the images on the screen. I noticed that in between shots of Nelson Mandela delivering a triumphant speech, there were shots of South Africa in general interspersed in the mix. There were children playing on dusty roads , but some appeared to not be wearing shoes, and they were entertaining them-selves with broken junk, like discarded bicycle rims and sticks. The thought pressed at me like an irreconcilable riddle: "How could they be walking on some of the richest soil in the world but not be able to afford shoes?" I strug-gled to douse the fires of cognitive dissonance that the scene had sparked in my mind, and finally, I began to ponder the possibility that vast sums and treasures were waiting for someone to unearth them and as though a perfect storm of realization had been summoned by my inner muse all at once, the flames of doubt were doused, and the beginnings of a plan began to sprout up from the ashes. In the back of my mind, reminiscent of Descartes' inspiring angel, a still small voice began to insist, "You have to go to Africa in search of gold and diamonds."

Enter Eli the drummer in my band, and one of my very close friends. The way I came to know Eli was a bit of a stroke of luck, maybe some would say fate. I was looking for a day gig. I happened to walk into a company that was located in the Eagle Bank building in South Miami; their name was Intercept America. The first hint that something was a little unusual about this place was the hiring manager. Picture someone with the long, black hair of a would-be Colombian rockstar. More than that, he was decked out in stage gear, like you had snatched a Latin David Lee Roth out of some alternate reality and slapped him behind a cubicle. Naturally, we started to get along immediately.

I soon found out that he and I had a band and one of the first things I told him was I think I'm going to be your new singer. Eli had discovered Intercept America via a newspaper ad. The company claimed that they were going to reinvent customer service by way of providing a virtual secretary that would replace human service representatives completely. The marketing pitch involved a lot of buzzwords concerning the nascent field of Artificial Intelligence (AI) and the dawn of the internet, and under very contrived circumstances, the product could even appear to actually work. At the end of the day, the machine they talked up so well amounted to little more than a glorified answering machine.

To cut a long story short, Intercept America was a company looking to defraud any investor they could get to ante up $50,000 or more, which Eli had in fact convinced someone to do, earning him a job as a branch manager. It was a well-organized professionally crafted front, and from the outside, it appeared to be a well funded and even a potentially visionary corporation that had begun to gather attention from hopeful technologists.

A good amount of investors were drawn in before the wheels started coming off of the whole thing. One day after hundreds of complaints to the Better Business Bureau, the FBI showed up, and only then did it become clear that it had been a scam as company leadership tried to take the money and run as it were.

Perhaps one of the reasons that Eli was able to pitch the concept so well was that he had bought into it himself. It turns out he had mortgaged his home and had invested $50,000 of his own money with Intercept America. Our rehearsal studio had been built in the backyard of that same home specifically for our band FarrCry. He was counting on that investment to help defend his father who was under investigation for piloting cocaine from Colombia. Of course, as a result of the FBI raiding Intercept America, Eli and I both were now unemployed.

As you might well imagine, I had no way to repay the $50,000 loan. Our only move was to stall the foreclosure procedures that would begin inevitably for as long as possible. The entire management staff of Intercept America had simply vacated upon the FBI's arrival. Everything was up for grabs, and Eli tried to get back as much of his $50,000 as he could by taking office furniture as well as computers. That's when I had the idea of sneaking into the server room and printing out their entire client list. While the machine had not worked, it had identified thousands of people in Miami with a need for that type of service, and I didn't know it at the time but this would turn out to be a very good idea and a very valuable list.

As far as I was concerned, we had a very good thing going on with the band—it's a type of chemistry that's very hard to find. We were becoming more and more focused on what we wanted to do. With the exception of my resolved issue with drinking and cocaine in the past there was never another substance abuse issue within the band. We had a very good work ethic. We rehearsed a lot, we were at the studio 6 days a week, and we wrote constantly. Everyone was allowed to write their own parts, and we had all agreed to split the writing. That seemed to shock a lot of people, but our philosophy was simple. If everyone were allowed to contribute evenly and only produce songs as a band then everyone would work for the best outcome each and every time. Also we wouldn't have problems with individuals insisting we did "their" song, even if it wasn't necessarily that good.

At any rate, the band comprised Eli, our drummer (whom you've already met), and then there was Craig, our guitar player, Ira, our keyboard player, and Randy. Randy was the last to join—he was the quintessential bass player. He was delivering pizzas for a living but he owned a small condo in Ft. Lauderdale, and was a hard worker and a very seasoned bass player on the cover circuit, but this was to be his first time performing original compositions.

I myself had come from a well known cover band, and it was going to be my first time writing and performing original material as well. Ira was a music major at the University of Miami, and he drove a Porsche, and that seemed to have been enough for Craig, who was the one who brought Ira into the band. Craig and Eli had already been practicing together for a couple of years when I came along.

The studio had been our haven. It represented an accomplishment for any band to have their own studio. After having started out in warehouses that were designed for storage and facing the array of problems that came along with those types of places, we were really happy when Eli had told us that he would be building it. It was just a 40' X 20' rectangle with a single door, and no windows. But it was solid concrete block construction with a hurricane-rated roof, and it was soundproofed. We could play as loud and as late as we wanted to and we did, and for the first few years, it was our home away from home.

Eli had taken a number of computers out of the Intercept America office space as well as some furniture. Their worth didn't come close to the 50K he had invested but I had a plan brewing in my head.

I had made a couple of trips to the library and was spending my Sundays reading everything I could find regarding mining for gold and diamonds in South Africa. Most of the material I was able to find at the time was pretty dated although it began to give me a back story on mining in South Africa, and it began to create a picture for me. The more I learned, the more fascinated I became.

One of the things I learned was that there were two types of mining. There is mining the ore—the kimberlite, as it's known, is the substrate in which diamonds are formed. The kimberlite pipes that contain the diamonds were pushed up during volcanic eruptions that occur beginning at great depth and pressure. Some of the pipes are large enough to drive a vehicle through.

Kimberlite pipes are most readily identifiable by their green or yellow color. Indeed the earliest miners of Kimberlite pipes in Kimberly, South Africa, simply referred to them as "blue ground" and "yellow ground," which were known to contain diamonds and other semi-precious stones. If a particular pipe yields a diamond or even samples well geologically for the potential to contain them, it is not uncommon for industrious miners to erect compounds demarcated by tall fences and guarded entry ways. Once vehicles enter, they are typically not allowed to leave without being searched. In some instances, the workers employed by the mine will be led to believe that they are being X-Rayed as they leave to discourage them from absconding with any stones they may have found.

The second type of mining is called alluvial mining and the easiest way to explain this type of mining is to say these are the diamonds that are spread in volcanic eruptions. Magmic flows coupled with other seismic disturbances brought on by the erupting volcano move these diamonds out of the kimberlite pipes and spread them into more accessible sediment layers. They can be found near riverbeds, and sometimes, even at surface level. Sieves and pans suffice to unearth the precious stones that have been thrust into alluvial soil, and lighter machinery can be employed to clear the land and move the earth. If you see people searching for diamonds with handheld tools, you can be sure they are alluvial miners.

Alluvial mining seemed like the way to go for me. I was very excited to learn this interesting fact. It seemed to me that in a real life situation, the alluvial mines and miners would be easier to approach.

During that time, I was doing my research on one of those computers that Eli had taken from Intercept America. Eli had, in fact, gifted it to me as he was becoming aware of my idea to try to find gold and diamonds somewhere in Africa.

This was the very beginning of the internet, and more technical knowledge of the POP3 and SMTP protocols was required to send and receive an email at that time than most students learn in Network Engineering 101 these days. Learning how to use it made me feel like I was thinking faster than the competition, whoever they might be. At that time, the entire bibliography of the public library system was indexed in a virtual dewey decimal system. You couldn't yet read books online but you could search for titles and know exactly what shelf they were sitting on in the library that housed them.

The most important and life-changing book I found this way was *The Diamond People* by Murray Shumach, and although it's really a murder story, I found invaluable snippets of information. With these little snippets, I began to paint a mental image of how the diamond industry operates. I learned that 90% of the world's quality gemstone is mined from a little African country called Sierra Leone, and those diamonds were recovered exclusively by alluvial mining. The concentration of precious stones and metals is so dense in that country that it's sometimes called The Athens of Africa.

Also, the internet afforded me the ability to receive real time state advisories from the government websites. From those advisories, I learned that Sierra Leone had 17 years of political stability.

I also learned that the French as well as the Russians had taken turns mining in Sierra Leone. All of the nice roads around Sierra Leone were said to have been built by the Russians, who had tried mining there. It was reported that after the Russians built out some infrastructure, the French began to take holidays in Freetown, and would buy matchboxes of diamonds in town. They would mostly receive industrial quality stones but on occasion, there was a true gem. This kept the tourists coming back for a long time.

Another interesting fact I discovered reading the book was that New York and Miami were large diamond districts. Miami had a new Metro rail system that ran from Kendall all the way to downtown Miami. The Seybold building specifically was known to be a large diamond district. So now I had my starting point. I would drive the green Volkswagen with no reverse to the station in Kendall and take the train all the way to downtown Miami. From there I would walk the few blocks to the Seybold building. I did not ever expect to be able to see a rough diamond but I did expect to be able to see all manner of cut and polished diamonds. Eli had procured a green American Express card with the FarrCry company name on it and had given me a duplicate card.

I knew absolutely nothing about diamonds but I began to pose as a buyer. In order to make the shopkeepers comfortable, I would flash the American Express card and let them know that that's how I would be paying. That turned out to be a bit of an embarrassment as any real diamond trader would know that it's a cash business and absolutely no one would use a credit card as I was about to learn. That *faux pas* turned out to be important in a way that I could never have predicted because that's how I got the attention of a diamond cutter known as Ygal Mannelis.

On one of these occasions, Ygal, a middle-aged Israeli man with copper-colored skin and a neatly trimmed beard pulled me to the side, and asked, "What are you really doing here? Anyone who's here to buy diamonds knows a credit card is no way to pay for them."

I'm sure I turned red but I decided at that moment that I had nothing to lose by telling someone with experience my idea. As Ygal considered what I was revealing about my plans, he nodded slowly, and when I was done speaking, he verified that he knew people whose business it was to smuggle diamonds out of Africa. He made a point of stressing that the journey would be full of difficulty and risk but that successful smugglers were by no means unheard of. What really excited me was that he proceeded to offer to teach me all I could absorb about rough stones, on the condition that should I ever make it to Sierra Leone, he would have the first pick of anything I returned with. He invited me to return to his office on Monday at ten. It was a very happy Metro Rail ride home.

Ygal had verified my idea, and even more than that seemed willing to invest time and effort into making sure I would be prepared with the knowledge I needed for a successful trip.

The Seybold building is the second largest hub for trading diamonds in the United States and the impressive ten story building hosts both artisans and vendors in the diamond and jewelry enterprises. Ygal had given me his business card, which had his office phone number and hours neatly printed under a banner in a custom font that read 'YNG Diamonds'. I noticed that his office was on the tenth floor. One had to pass through security in order to ride the elevator that went to the tenth floor.

That Monday, in Ygal's office was the first time I ever saw a rough diamond. They were of course amazing, and he was showing me some very big stones; eight-sided stones, these were considered to be completely finished forming—not every diamond is. They come in several forms. Ygal elucidated the differences between the types of rough stones and the various shapes that they could be cut into, showing me examples of each if they were handy. He went on to teach me the color scale that diamonds are graded by, the topology of finished stones and anything else he thought I might need for a gemology crash course that would soon be put to test in the wild.

I spent the next ten months going to see Ygal at least once a week, sometimes a couple of times. Each time I learned something new. You maybe wouldn't think it, but there is a lot to learn. There remained one rather large problem. Where would I get the funds to finance not only the trip but the discretionary funds with which to purchase rough once I made it to Africa?

Almost a year had passed since the debacle that was Intercept America. The whole thing seemed to fade away the same way it had arrived. Eli heard nothing more from the investigators who had been asking him questions on the day of the raid. In fact he hadn't heard anything at all. And that was good in one way. I had been worried a bit that there would be a record of me having printed the client list that Intercept America had collected pitching their product to anyone that might want it.

I was also worried that the security cameras had seen me, and I knew the FBI was looking at everything. In the end, I wasn't ever even interviewed. There were dozens and dozens of people who had been there longer than me. I guess they figured they had heard the same story about how folks had come to find this job enough times.

I had kept that client list, and now I was thinking it was time to find out what it might be worth.

I went to see the owner of a pretty well known answering service that I will not name in order to avoid any legal trouble for myself going forward or any embarrassment for the company that purchased the list, but I will say that I am glad to see that they rapidly grew even bigger and are still in business today.

The sale of the list was relatively easy, I was given an office for a couple of days, and I asked them to provide me random samples of the names on the client list. I then set to prove the value of the list by calling the names given to me, and employing a pitch similar to the one taught to me by Intercept America, seizing on the knowledge that I was somehow aware that they had had a bad experience with their last company but that this company was the real deal. And that's all it took. I sold a dozen clients a day in no time.

I'll never really know how much the list was worth to them. But they paid me 14K dollars for it. Beggars can't be choosers, and I was pretty happy to have turned it at all.

That still wasn't enough money to fund the buying but it covered the price of the trip and still left about 9k in the roll.

I was thinking that I needed a cover story for traveling to Sierra Leone. Also I was worried about personal safety, and I couldn't take a chance on carrying a concealed weapon, especially not in a country like Sierra Leone. Even though I hadn't yet been there, I'd always been aware of the dangers that might exist in third world country jails and hospitals.

It didn't appear that anyone was too willing to go into the jungles of Sierra Leone with me. In fact one of the things I heard the most as I was planning my excursion was that if it were that easy, everyone would be doing it. And people said that with such conviction, it's a wonder I didn't begin to question myself or believe them.

Ira Salzman was our keyboard player, and was the last member to come into the band. I never attempted to delve into his private life, I knew that Ira had lost both of his parents by the time he came to us. He was answering an ad that Craig had placed in *Rag* magazine, looking for a keyboard player. Craig had liked him and wanted the rest of us to meet him so he invited him to our rehearsal studio and the rest was history, we all took to each other and the chemistry was good.

Ira had once told me that his mom had passed due to skin cancer. He had said that it wasn't long at all between diagnosis and her death. The cancer had metastasized to her lymph nodes.

I believe his dad had a heart attack sometime after his mom's passing. He was not an only child; he had a brother and a sister, both older.

I knew he had received a large inheritance of some sort but only because of the obvious signs like going through cars like they were free—one week he was driving a Porsche, the next a Lotus, the next a Corvette, then a Nissan Z, then a Lexus. The list goes on and on, and of course, he always lived in very nice places. So at this particular point in time, he was living in a penthouse apartment in Aventura Florida at a very posh place called The Waterway.

I figured that Ira had as much love for the band as I did, and that it was as important to him as it was to me. I had not told Eli of my idea to ask Ira for a loan so we could get our studio out of the path of the proverbial boulder-sized eight ball. So it came as quite the shock that morning in his penthouse kitchen with the dazzling view of the city of Aventura as well as the Atlantic ocean, when he suggested we should fire Eli and replace him rather than risk going off to Africa to smuggle diamonds. Because "If it were that easy, everyone would be doing it"

That morning was a bit of a wake-up call for me. I really believed in "one for all and all for one" to the point that risking life, freedom, or limb seemed like an easy choice. I know I had been very careful to never ask or rely on Ira for money because I didn't ever want him to think that he was only in the band because he appeared to have money. I mean we had one guy who delivered pizzas for a living and another who was a trust fund baby, and the rest of us somewhere in between. But I always wanted things to be even within the band as much as possible. That's why I made sure all royalties related to writing and publishing were shared evenly in fifths.

It was also very important to me to not ever ask Ira for any sum of money though it was obvious he had it. However, on this occasion, when one of our best friends was in jeopardy *and* our rehearsal location and essentially business headquarters was at risk as well; I was not expecting at all the callous suggestion to simply fire Eli and let him worry about his own problems. I didn't even end up asking him for the help I wanted; I just expressed my unwavering intent to get diamonds out of the jungle, out of which would come a year's worth of money for me to invest into turning myself into America's favorite son, and the proceeds to rescue our studio that happened to be in arrears.

Not long after that one night after practice, the band decided to take a walk along South Beach. We just needed a break, and it was something we were known to do every once in a while. If things at the studio were not clicking, we would decide to go to the movies together or take a walk, and oftentimes, it helped to get us out of a rut, past one thing or another. But on this night I met a girl. It seemed to me like from a distance we had both simultaneously noticed each other and I was drawn to go talk to her. Her name was Shirley. And as it turned out, she was a singer working nights in the Grove. She was also a bartender on South Beach, trying to make ends meet. At any rate, Shirley and I started talking, and we began to see each other more regularly. She would sometimes meet me at my apartment after rehearsal and she would spend the night.

It wasn't long before I revealed to her what I had been planning. I knew she had to be in good shape for obvious reasons but also we would go on 2 and 3 mile runs, and she could always keep up. I had fortunately been a long-time runner, and had done breathing exercises for years in an attempt to improve my singing voice. One night, after a pretty grueling 3 mile run, which we finished in just under a half-hour, Shirley began to express an interest in going to Africa with me.

She told me how she used to work on an ocean-going catamaran that groups would rent for fishing and sailing trips. She said that as part of the liveaboard crew, she had had her experiences in dealing with drunk guys out at sea, and how she had always managed to diffuse or derail tense and possibly dangerous situations. I had no reason to doubt her stories or her convictions about her own self-assuredness and level-headedness.

She even gave me a great idea regarding a safe but effective weapon we could carry without fear of breaking the law. A stun gun. They were a relatively new thing for average citizens, and maybe people wouldn't be too aware of what they were and if they were discovered, we could claim they were just strobe lights for photography, and that we in fact were just wildlife photographers. And just like that, the cover story took shape. Shirley was in—she would be my accomplice.

Phones with cameras had not yet been invented but I found a couple of 35mm cameras in a pawn shop. They had telescoping lenses, and I thought they looked the part. The stun guns I was able to acquire at a place that had just opened in Fort Lauderdale called the 'Spy Shop'. They had quite the amazing display of tasers and stun guns. We bought two of the most powerful ones they had. This weapon was pretty serious. It looked like it could double as a clip for an assault rifle, and it curved slightly like the blade of a scimitar. At the press of a button, lightning danced between the twin two-inch steel poles protruding from the top, like a barely contained force of nature.

I had the opportunity to see this little spectacle in action once, which I'll tell you about later.

It was a time of great excitement for me as we gathered the things that we thought we would need as well as procured passports, travel medicine, shots, airline and hotel reservations. With the computer, we would log in late at night on my Netscape account, which billed my credit card $17.50 an hour for the privilege of getting state travel advisories.

We were also able to locate maps and books through the computer, and then pick them up or scan them at the library, but it seemed a big help to be able to search the library from home essentially, and to know what you were picking up and where in the library it was located once you got there.

We now knew we were headed to the capital of Sierra Leone, Freetown. So named because during the Revolutionary War, this was the reentry point for many slaves that had allied with the British returning home from America by way of Nova Scotia, as well as those slaves that were liberated by the British from America during the conflict. Thanks to the books and the maps, we could see that we would be arriving at an island just off the coast of Freetown, called Lungi. From Lungi, we knew we would have to board a ferry to cross the bay to Freetown, where we could catch a cab to the hotel, which was known locally as the Mammy Yoko Hotel named after a female leader of the Mende tribe renowned for her skill with bladed weapons and shrewd tactics in battle and negotiations alike.

So having acquired all the necessary travel documents and the inoculations that were mandatory before traveling to certain regions of the world, Shirley and I were ready to go. We chose to travel from Atlanta to Holland on KLM Airlines. We had decided to fly business class, and I'm glad we did. The entire trip would encompass about 30 hours of travel, and the amenities offered in business class would be the last bits of comfort for a couple of weeks anyway. From Holland, we would continue on KLM airlines direct to Sierra Leone.

CHAPTER 2

W e arrived on a Thursday night, and I remember this because there was only one KLM flight a week, and it came on Thursdays—so minimum stay would always be at least one week.

Arriving in Sierra Leone is an experience I'll never forget—it's the closest I've ever felt to stepping out of a time machine. As we descended metal stairs down towards the tarmac, two things struck me simultaneously. One was a chorus of jungle sounds, and the other was this odd smell—a mixture of ocean and papaya and also body odor. These folks were apparently not big on deodorants. If you ever go there yourself, you will remember having read this paragraph. At any rate, it's something that you get used to rather quickly as there is a lot of commotion when this flight arrives. It's like a weekly happening that brings opportunity to the locals. The airport was on an island after all, and the ferry that transported new arrivals to the main land of the country was too far from the airport to walk, so everyone would need a cab. There were bags to carry, and plenty of foreigners tipping in their own currencies. Guides presented themselves almost immediately, and even the customs agents were tipped well. It was all part of an underlying diamond culture that everyone tried to get a little piece of. Something I would come to understand better and better over time.

Shirley had secured me a second loan, and in the end, Ira had a change of heart as he lent Eli another $5K, which he had promptly given to me. I now had a total of $25k, most of which was in a money belt that was strapped around my waist. I had not anticipated needing as much cash just to get through the airport as it took. As we approached customs, each with our duffle bags, we came to a wooden table with a customs officer standing behind it. We each put our bags on the table expecting to be searched and to explain all the "photo gear" but instead, he just said "That's eighty dollars." Not having had this type of experience in the past, I exclaimed perhaps a little loudly "For what?" He just looked at me, and in a heavy accent, he said, "This is your first trip to Sierra Leone." And the look he was giving said everything else I needed to know, so I paid him $40 per bag, and he marked each of them with a blue piece of chalk.

I only had another twenty left in free floating cash, so I needed to find a restroom where I could open the money belt. Unfortunately all traffic moves in one direction, and there were no facilities at the Arrival Wing. I was forced to untuck the belt and slide the pocket that held the money from my back to my front at waist level so I could unzip it and retrieve a couple of bills. Having done this as quickly and discreetly as possible, I quickly noticed that I had been seen by at least a couple of people, one who asked me right away if I needed a cab. Things were moving a little too quickly.

I was aware that Shirley was nearby, and I said yes to the cab offer, at which point the man began to wave his hand over my head as if to indicate to someone to come get us, and sure enough, up pulled a car, which bore no resemblance to a cab other than it was a car. The guy who had summoned the car was quickly placing our duffle bags in the trunk. Shirley and I got in the back seat after I had tipped him. The driver then had a quick conversation with the man in a dialect that I couldn't understand.

As we pulled away from the airport area in the back of this impromptu cab, I hate to admit it but the cliché, 'I don't think we're in Kansas anymore', sprung to mind. The roads out of Lungi airport are red clay to this day. They are narrow and surrounded by deep palm jungles. We had arrived late in the afternoon, and the sun was retreating behind the horizon as we meandered down foreign paths piloted by someone we didn't know into the dimly receding twilight.

There were no street lights and no lights to be seen either in front of us or behind us. Then I began to notice that there was no traffic behind us and none ahead either. Some dwellings could be seen sporadically along the path and they resembled shanties more than proper dwellings. We passed a large

55 gallon drum, which contained a fire, and there were a few women standing around it, all of them topless. Some turned to gaze at us as we passed, others seemed to ignore us completely.

At about that moment, it began to occur to me that I had no idea where we were, and that for all I knew, we were being driven to some secluded spot, where our heads would be summarily hacked off with a machete and the 25 grand I had naively revealed would be their prize.

We had been in the country less than an hour, and already I had somehow screwed it up by revealing the money and hopping into a stranger's vehicle without question in the heat of the moment. A deep sense of impending danger motivated me to action.

I moved forward in my seat directly behind the driver, and slipped my arm over the headrest and under his throat putting him into a tight chokehold, his head immobile, and his arms ill-placed to strike back at me.

"Stop the car, or I'll strangle you in your seat." He stopped the car and I demanded of him as bravely as possible for someone who was more than half sure he was about to be robbed in the jungle, "Where are we going? Why are there no other people behind or ahead of us? Wouldn't we all be going towards the same ferry?"

Shirley was turning white, and her eyes were the size of dinner plates. The driver began to explain that perhaps we had been the last to leave, and that when the ferry arrived, they would start the generator, which powered the lights. He went on to say that they don't keep it running because of the cost of the fuel. "I promise you, sir, they will come on!"

I responded that we would just sit there then and wait to see if he was telling the truth. It was a very tense couple of minutes that passed in complete silence. But sure enough, eventually, lights could be seen emerging further up the dark road, and as vehicles got off the ferry, they began heading in the direction from which we had just come.

I apologized to the driver profusely. He seemed no worse for the wear, and I tipped him generously, whipping fifties off the top of the money roll as I apologized bashfully. I did have to suffer the embarrassment of hearing him tell the story to a fellow cabbie on the ferry, and they both seemed to get a good laugh out of it.

The ferry reached the dock in Freetown, and even in the dark of the night, I could tell I was in a place that was very different from what I had been accustomed to. The 55-gallon drums that were on every other street corner lit the places where the electric was either out, which was frequently, or there wasn't any to begin with. The open street sewers provided a very unwanted fragrance, most of the homes were dilapidated and they appeared flimsy and were mostly made of wood and corrugated tin.

The streets seemed to criss-cross randomly, like they were laid on a whim or perhaps dwellings had simply sprung up organically along ancient foot-paths. Occasionally, there would be a home built of concrete blocks that would dominate a particular street, and all the surrounding dwellings were essentially shacks at irregular intervals. There was a large modern football stadium that seemed to be the pride and joy of Freetown that contrasted starkly with the otherwise mostly ruinous architecture. Of course, the Mammy Yoko hotel and its satellite buildings, including a little bar much frequented by foreigners of a diamond-seeking persuasion or otherwise was another major exception. Their power was always on as they had large generators and fuel storage that the locals were not fortunate enough to enjoy in their homes. This little bar even makes an appearance in the movie *Blood Diamond*. As our driver made a turn off the coastal highway onto a side street towards the Mammy Yoko's front entrance, we immediately noticed that the hotel was behind a large gate in what appeared to be a compound. Only cabs carrying passengers from the airport were allowed to enter, and if a guest wanted a cab, one would be summoned from outside the gate.

The hotel itself was unremarkable, and very average. There was, as you might expect, an eclectic array of colorful people, citizens of other African countries, who wore traditional dress, mingled among French and American tourists and businessmen.

Checking in was uneventful, and Shirley and I were happy to be at the hotel. We had been traveling for about 30 hours straight, with maybe a few hours' sleep on the first transatlantic flight but none since then. We washed up quickly and hastily got into bed.

The bright tropical sunshine filtering through the window awoke me the next morning. Here I was finally in Sierra Leone after a year of planning. I looked at Shirley waking up next to me and realized this was the extent of my plan. I still didn't have any idea of how I would find the diamonds. I knew it was illegal to purchase them. Diamonds of a certain weight and size automatically became the property of the government. And it was widely rumored that the Central Intelligence Division would frequently set up unknowing buyers.

The way the trick worked was that a seller would approach a buyer in the hotel. Usually, he would offer to sell the illicit diamond to the buyer, who would agree, and think themselves so lucky to have located such a large stone without even leaving the hotel. The price would be fair, which should be your first warning that something was not right. But of course, the unsuspecting buyer paid for the stone, then the seller informed the CID of the buyer's room number, and they would come and seize the stone while letting the buyer know they were doing him the favor of keeping his money as a fee for avoiding prosecution for violating Sierra Leone's diamond laws, Then they would turn around and do it again to the next uninformed diamond buyer. This was a typical case of 'if it's too good to be true…' A good rule of thumb for anyone looking to try their hand at diamond smuggling is: don't do business with people who approach you without you initiating the contact.

We decided to see what was available from the hotel by the way of excursions. That would at least be a start and get us acclimated with the town's layout. I headed down to the lobby where on the way in I had spotted a sign that offered jeep and helicopter tours.

There, in a corner of the lobby, was a glass office with a small sign that read 'Tours' mounted above it. The office was occupied by a young woman of about 30; she was smartly dressed and wore glasses. Her name was Pauline.

I was able to schedule a tour of Freetown for Shirley and me for a little later that morning by jeep. I went back to the room to get Shirley and apprise her of our plan for the day. We grabbed the cameras and the telephoto lenses as well as a camera bag with other accessories including the stun gun well, prepared to play the part of wild-life photographers.

When we came back down to the lobby, we rode down the elevator with a French couple, who did not speak to us even as we greeted them and they ignored us again when we bid them good day upon exiting the elevator.

I thought we were going to be in for a long day if they were going on the tour with us. I was relieved to see that they were not but I was a bit surprised that Shirley and I were the only two people on the tour. The tour had been a good idea, as it gave us a chance to see Freetown in the daylight for the first time. There were points of interest, like a dilapidated television station that the Russians had built, but it was non-operational for lack of "parts" also the guide took us to the city's fresh water treatment facility that desalinated the ocean water for clean drinking water.

There was also an old monastery that had been there for a very long time. All of these things I can tell you nothing about, as my mind was on one thing and one thing only that whole day. The diamonds. The one thing that I did notice was that the guide never brought up the diamond trade at all. And finally, towards the end of the tour, I asked where the diamonds that I'd heard so much about might be found. He seemed genuinely uncomfortable as he stammered that the diamond fields were "up-country," far from Freetown but he had no knowledge outside of that. It was clear though from his change in demeanor that he either really didn't want to talk about the diamond fields or couldn't talk about them for some reason. But I had heard the term "up-country" for the first time, and now I knew it was a destination, a real place and a place that I had to find out more about.

That first day was going well until what was supposed to be the last stop of the tour. The jeep stopped at the bottom of a gravel hill that we were supposed to walk up in order to get this great view of the ocean and the sunset. It was quite beautiful I must say, stunning really, and would have been worth the while if not for Shirley taking a fall as we descended.

The gravel was loose and her feet just slid out from under her, and as she went to her butt she put her hand down to break her fall. In doing so, she dislocated her thumb. I was able to reset it but it had quickly begun to swell. Shirley did not want to seek medical help there, and I can't say I blamed her. We headed back to the hotel to get her hand in some ice.

We had brought some Advil and I was able to get a bucket of ice for her hand. But she was done for the night and said she didn't want to go back out that night. I told her I understood and we agreed I should go alone.

I decided to take a camera and acquaint myself with Freetown. I quickly learned there were a lot of people who felt that if you took a picture of them, you might be attempting to forge a type of link to their soul through their image that could be used to affect magical harm. Why else would you need such a representation of them?

One of the harrowing realities of life in Sierra Leone is the abysmal child mortality rate. Only one in five children made it past the age of five. A combination of disease, malnutrition and violence had imposed a type of weakness filter on those that did survive the odds. As a result of this, almost everyone appeared to be in incredible physical shape despite the lack of adequate nutrition or gyms. I was about thirty feet away from someone who was engaged in a household chore in his front yard but boasted a physique that would usually belong to someone who had spent decades training in the West. I snapped a quick photo of him. Suddenly he pivoted in my direction, and locked eyes with me. "You're American, aren't you?" he asked, to which I replied yes. "It's all over you," he said. Aside from my long hair, I thought I resembled the average foreign photographer. At the time, I didn't understand his meaning but I decided against taking any further pictures of people without their consent. That pretty much sums up my first twenty four hours in Freetown.

Returning to the hotel, I found Shirley still icing her injured thumb and still in no mood to leave the hotel room. I guess that Sierra Leone wasn't living up to her expectations or to her comparisons of catamaran sailing in the Caribbean.

I went down to the restaurant to get us both something to eat. I can't really remember what we had for dinner that night but the food at the hotel was not as appetizing as we expected it might be, and we were being cautious with what we ate and drank.

I know I wasn't being great company to Shirley as my mind was on the diamond business, I just wasn't sure how I would find anyone who was dealing illicit diamonds. The next day I made my way into town alone again as Shirley appeared to be getting worse, and I don't mean her hand. Her attitude was changing. She seemed to have lost interest in the plan, and I hadn't seen her smile since we had arrived.

I made my way to the marketplace that was in the center of town, it was a bazaar, like a giant flea market, however, the wares were a bit different. Here there were pelts and snake skins, and many other things like clothes and boots for sale. I was very dismayed to find a gorilla hand, which had been fashioned into an ashtray. There was hardware on sale such as generators, shovels, axes, machetes. It was quite busy actually, and the hustle and bustle had a positive energy to it. I came upon one vendor who was selling stone sculptures that had been made with hammer and chisel. Another vendor had some very intricate wood carvings, both the stone and wood art mostly depicted stylized faces of heroes, warriors, and local deities. I began asking one of these shopkeepers if they had any diamonds to sell, and even though the answer was 'no' every time, the way in which some of them said 'no' let me know that I was at least close to something. Some of the vendors seemed half scared and half annoyed by the request, while others just seemed scared.

I knew there had to be a culturally acceptable way to broach the subject, but either I wasn't asking the right way or I wasn't asking the right people. I felt so close to my goal, and so far away, I wished with all my strength to discern that special combination of words and perhaps a wink or other gesture that would let them know I was offering a serious opportunity and it was worth the trouble of revealing things best left unspoken to most visitors. I made my way back to the beach side of the Mammy Yoko. Just up the road from the hotel beach was a beach bar I mentioned earlier. I asked the bartender if there was any truth to the rumor I had just made up regarding someone nearby who could find diamonds for sale. But unlike the movies, the answer was yet another "no" accompanied by a stern warning from the bartender that I was likelier to be killed or arrested or both than make a successful find. He warned of the scam artists and of corrupt police. There was a second hotel on that beach; it was quite nice and offered beach bunga-lows. As I walked along, I saw a monkey who was chained to a tree. He appeared to be the equivalent of the parrots sometimes kept at Caribbean resorts. He was well-fed and appeared more or less happy with his existence, but he was no help locating diamonds either. It was getting late and I headed back to the hotel where I came upon Pauline, who was just closing the tour office for the day. She gave a cheerful hello and inquired about the tour—she had left by the time we returned, so I told her we found it informative and very enjoyable overall. I mentioned that Shirley had slipped at the very last stop and had spent yesterday and today in the room nursing her hand. Pauline said she was sorry to hear of the mishap and offered her assistance. If there was anything she could do to make it better, Shirley and I should let her know, she insisted. I thanked her and when she said goodbye, she sounded very genuine and kind.

When I returned to the room I told Shirley what the day had been like as well as what Pauline had just said. Her air of indifference had worsened if anything, and there were four days left until the next flight. I was starting to worry a bit. As if it wasn't hard enough finding a diamond dealer, I was now beginning to worry about Shirley, and starting to think she was not much help, which I suppose, I could forgive. But she was becoming a hindrance—a negative presence—with no input and not even the capacity to be a sound-ing board. I knew her hand was probably aching and throbbing but still her reaction seemed extreme.

Even though I had not yet voiced this fear, I had no plan beyond this point. I didn't know what I would tell Eli or how we would be able to continue our efforts as musicians back home or how I would even pay rent next month.

We went to sleep that night without saying a word. Television, by the way, was non-existent, the hotel had no closed circuit video offerings and we already knew the one television station in Freetown was non-operational. So to sit in the room all day was literally to just sit in silence. At least the room had a balcony with a nice view of the beach and the pool area. There was live music coming from the bar on the beach at night; there was a jukebox and Janet Jackson's *Black Cat* seemed to be a crowd favorite.

I woke up with a sense of urgency on the 4th day. There were 3 days to departure, and I hadn't even seen a diamond. It occurred to me that in four days, I hadn't even met anyone—no one at all—except for Pauline, that is. I don't know what drove me to take a chance inside the hotel but I approached Pauline that morning, and that was going to be both the best and worst day of that trip. Pauline said that she herself did not know but thought that her husband might as he was a businessman in town and he ran a newspaper press, so he knew many people from different walks of life in Sierra Leone. Both Pauline and her husband Harry had studied in the UK and returned to Freetown. I explained my urgency as the flight was once a week, and Shirley's condition was going to prevent her from staying another week. Her hand was indeed hurt, and as it turned out, she did need surgery to fix it properly. More on that in a moment. She couldn't make any promises and I understood how things moved at a certain pace there, but nonetheless, I wondered if I could possibly meet Harry that day. She said she would call him at his press and ask his schedule. This wasn't much at all. Obviously, but it was all I had, and it was the first conversation in four days that hadn't ended with a no.

I took the elevator up to our floor to tell Shirley the good news, but when I entered the room, I found Shirley sitting on the bed with my travel documents, and she seemed pretty angry. I nonetheless tried to tell her I had at least met someone who was married to someone who might know of someone who might sell diamonds. I know that hearing it now, it seems so scant, so impossibly little, to expect anyone else to put as much stock in my maybe meeting as I did, but I already knew that sometimes in life you have to will things into existence. It would be easy to say we failed, everyone was right, if it were that easy everyone would be doing it, but I just couldn't.

I had to prove them wrong, if only just because people can be so smug when they try to write you off. Nothing was going to conquer Shirley's bad mood. She launched into a tirade about how I had not talked about anything other than diamonds since we left Miami. She was sick of this "Devil Business," and she wanted nothing more to do with it. I hadn't spoken a romantic word in all the time we had been alone on this trip. And that was all true but it was also the plan, and diamonds were the primary reason for our being here. She had begun to get a little loud so I suggested she come with me and get out of this room that she'd been locked in for over three days without so much as a radio. I convinced her that she had a bad case of cabin fever and she needed some air. I ushered her out of the room. We walked down the hall to the elevator and as we entered, I sent the elevator to the roof instead of to the lobby. There were bound to be people in the lobby, and we certainly didn't want to be screaming about this devil business in the lobby. Also, I had already been to the roof for a moment and noticed it had a great view and was even set up for guests to enjoy it. But as we stepped out and Shirley noticed we had gone to the roof, she began to have another tirade, and it went something like this. "So this is it? This is where it happens?" she started accusatorily. "This was your plan all along. I found the papers. I know your plan, the life insurance, all of it! This is where you throw me off the roof to collect the insurance! I knew when I saw you with the cab driver that you had a dark side capable of killing but I didn't think you'd kill me..."

I guess I had had a rough week myself, and had been pretty occupied with the task of finding what we had come for. I suppose I might be the one who seemed distant, perhaps steadying myself to do her in, leaving her alone everyday in order to distance myself. But no, that hadn't been the case at all. I had been looking for someone to illegally sell me illicit diamonds at dirt cheap prices like I had told her I was.

I just went over to one of the lounge chairs and as all of the realizations of what she was thinking hit me, I just began to laugh. I honestly don't think I had ever laughed so hard before. It was as if I was on mushrooms and had heard the funniest joke ever; my eyes were tearing up and I doubled over in uncontrollable laughter. Soon Shirley began to laugh as well. And as her own realizations hit her and she heard how absurd that murder accusation sounded, suddenly we were both laughing like a couple of lunatics. When we finally did stop, and we were both just looking at each other, she asked, "But why the secrecy?" I hadn't meant to be secretive. I didn't want to seem morbid but I had taken out not only life insurance, but medical insurance, evacuation insurance, trip cancellation insurance, and I had taken it upon myself to make Eli the beneficiary if something should happen to us. In retrospect, I should have either asked her or excluded her from the insurance or named her mother as her beneficiary as she herself pointed out. In doing that, I was wrong, and Shirley, if you read this book, I apologize.

After that, she seemed to calm down about the insurance at least. She still continued to be spooked about the diamond seeking. I told her about Pauline and Harry, and how it was at least a shot in the dark but we had come all this way and time was running short.

As we entered our room, we saw that there was a note on the floor that had been slid under the door. It was from Pauline—the meeting with her husband would be that evening. That seemed to inspire Shirley a bit, and I was able to convince her to go with me.

After Pauline closed her shop in the hotel lobby for the evening, Shirley and I accompanied her home. There did not seem to be a middle class in Freetown but Harry and Pauline did appear to be so. Harry was a slight fellow, maybe 5' 9", very trim. He was clean-shaven, and wore a shirt and tie every day. He looked every bit the part of a small business owner. He was soft-spoken and he appeared to be very calm and low-key. They lived in one of the few block construction homes that we saw; the house could have been in a neighborhood in South Miami or in Hialeah, Florida. It was the typical 2 bed 3 bath home you find there, complete with the wrought iron gates over the windows, and a small tile porch, which is where we spent the evening talking.

Harry said the power was only on intermittently, and when it was on, they had to hurry and make use of it for things like ironing shirts, using the stove, allowing the water heater to heat up. At least they had a water heater, not every home did. They, of course, had no television, but also there was no refrigerator. They did have an ice box, which was better than nothing but only if there was power to make ice. They did have a working phone that was independent of the power lines, and they said it was much more reliable.

This was a couple with two good jobs and a home—they were far better off than most. We talked about a lot of things. One of the things I still remember is Pauline telling me how surprised they both were in Europe when they first saw food that was canned for dogs, and cats too. But they said for some reason it was the dog food that provided a bit of their culture shock as they studied abroad. They did not want to bring children into this plight and had decided against having any.

I saw the need, and thought I should consider offering them a finder's fee if they could put me in touch with a diamond dealer from the up-country. There were only two full days left, and I thought it might be a good idea to send Shirley home and extend my stay by another week. Harry accepted my offer, and out of the money I had reserved for buying diamonds, I paid them $500. I deliberately took the money out of the money belt, revealing the two bricks to both of them. I offered them another $500 if I was able to make a buy from Harry's connection.

We agreed to return to the hotel and wait for Harry's call. The phone rang in the room at about 2 am; it was Harry and he said he was sure there would be a man coming from the up-country, who would have rough stones for sale, and that he would seek to make contact again first thing in the morning. There were only two nights left at the hotel but for the first time I fell asleep with some hope. The next morning, I was up early and down in the lobby for some coffee when I saw Pauline arriving for work. I went to greet her with a good morning and she asked me to come in a moment. She had a message from Harry, who had not wanted to speak in detail over the telephone. The meeting, if set, would probably be dangerous, and now that she had an idea of how much cash I was carrying, she wanted me to be aware that people had been killed here for infinitely less. I assured her I would be very careful, but it was a look she gave just as I shook her hand goodbye that concerned me.

Back at the room with a couple of coffees, I was about to ask Shirley how she felt about going back alone tomorrow if the meeting fell through. But the phone rang and hope swelled in my chest when I heard the tone in Harry's voice. He remained soft-spoken as ever but I could hear that he was pleased with himself, and he informed me that he had set up a meeting for this evening just after sundown. He added that he had seen the goods and that he had a car in which he would take me to the meeting. I started to get very excited about finding and seeing rough that had just been mined here in the up-country and brought down into Freetown, just like a story in one of the books about diamonds that I had read back in the States. It felt pretty good for some reason.

As evening approached, I got ready to go. I probably stuck out like a sore thumb. I had very long hair at the time, about 3/4th of the way down my back. I was wearing a red cap with my hair in a ponytail, jeans and snakeskin cowboy boots. I carried a small bag—it was actually a nylon travel bag I had gotten free with some purchase or other for the trip. That thought struck me as slightly ironic as I put twenty grand into that bag along with a pack of cigarettes, a lighter, my loupe, the diamond tester and the tazers. I guess I thought if things went wrong, two tasers might be better than one, and Shirley had no intention of leaving the room anyway.

Harry pulled up to the front lobby doors in an old but clean Nissan. I got in the passenger side and Harry drove us out the gate. That night I had the feeling that it was showtime—the same sense of anticipation that would permeate the atmosphere right before a groundbreaking performance as the crowd gathered. If there had been a downside to showing Harry the money last night, it was that right now he would know that I was carrying it. But I figured the fact that Shirley and his wife were still back at the hotel would prevent him from doing anything rash.

I tried to memorize the way there but that's not my strong suit. The drive took almost 40 minutes, so all I knew now was that we were far away from the Mammy Yoko. But I figured I'd got Harry and he wasn't going anywhere without his other $500. So I should be safe. I was wrong.

We arrived at an imposing 3-story concrete structure. I couldn't discern whether it was once an office building, a hotel, or a mansion but it was crumbling and ruinous. From the sidewalk, it looked like the last place on earth you would willingly walk into. As soon as I stepped out of the car, I was nearly overwhelmed by the oppressive stench of a nearby open sewer. Immediately, two men emerged from the rectangular, murky cavity that was once the doorway into this place. They had been expecting us. As they approached me, I looked to Harry to make an introduction, but Harry was still in the car peeking at me through cracked windows. "Go, it's okay. I'll be right here," he said.

Without a word of introduction or so much as a nod of acknowledgment, one of the men nudged me towards the stone steps of the entryway. They each turned on a flashlight, which revealed the silhouetted rifles each of them had slung over their shoulders. The weapons appeared to be Russian machine guns. I don't know guns well enough to tell you the model but I've seen it in movies—they have that curving banana clip. As we passed into the stuffy gloom of the saturnine edifice, I was again communicated with via the kinetic language of a nudge towards an old wooden staircase that was immediately to the right of the entrance. As I took my first steps up the creaking planks, my adrenaline went into overdrive.

My heart hammered in my ears, and I couldn't decide if this meant I felt more excited to be inches away from the riches I had traveled so far for, or terrified at the possibility of becoming one of the lost souls shrieking in the staircase. The way forward was barely illuminated by the flashlights and I was navigating by outline and guts, attempting to appear sure of my steps. They had me walking in the front, and all of the sudden, just for a moment, exhilaration morphed into a near primal panic. I think I heard one of the banana clips catch the concrete wall long ago denuded of its wallpaper, and something about it reminded me that this was not a dream, or an action movie. Somehow I had found myself in a slum rivaling Mogadishu with rifles inches from my back in the hands of men who had probably used them. My hands began to tremble noticeably but only for a moment; a survival instinct kicked in and that same still small voice made it clear that if I let these men see any fear, any sign that I wasn't completely in control of myself that I wouldn't be walking back down these same stairs. Something about the weight of that realization steadied my hands, and I decided to treat this like a performance, like a game, like it was just another night navigating some bar in Tampa, where they didn't like long-haired rockers.

Eventually, after going up another floor, we arrived at the one room in the building with light shining through the cracks in the door.

One of the armed men passed me and opened the door and the other followed close behind, kind of shepherding me in. A single bear bulb hung from the center of the ceiling. You could hear the hum of the generator that was powering it outside. The first rifle-toting escort to enter acknowledged an individual seated cross-legged on a sofa before a small table. From his sofa, the apparent leader of the cadre enjoyed the view outside the window. I was motioned to sit in a rather squat chair opposite him which put the window to my back. Then the two armed men took positions just across the room behind him, both assuming a quasi-military stance with legs spread wide apart and rifles pointing diagonally towards the ceiling—better than being pointed at me, I thought.

Neither of us spoke at first. For an awkward moment, the only sound in the room was the hum of the generator. I examined him closely; the seam of his robe was embroidered with an alternating pattern of white and blue squares from the nape of his neck straight down to his stomach. The robe had a breast-pocket that shared the same pattern down its middle. Deep set, slightly blood-shot eyes gazed back at me unwaveringly past a nose that took up a considerable amount of the real estate of this man's face. He sucked his lips together in what I assume was a sound of suspicion or contempt.

"Your friend tells me you are here in search of a diamond broker?" he asked.

"That's true, might you be the broker I've been looking for?" I countered.

He replied by producing from his robe's breast pocket the same blue paper with the wax lining that the Israeli diamond dealers in Miami used. It's a small world. He unwrapped the paper which contained three individual parcels, each of which, he said, had to be purchased together. The display was quite impressive. I don't know how much money Harry had told them I looked to be carrying but there was about $100K of value represented by the rough stones in front of me. I didn't even need the diamond tester. Here were some exquisite rough diamonds right out of a best case scenario find most of them fully formed. Very few stood out as slightly below grade compared to the beauties they were sitting next to.

The reason the stones were separated into parcels was in order for them to be able to sell the slightly less desirable stones as well as the nice ones. It was a common practice; I had learned and it did not come as any sort of surprise.

The bulb flickered occasionally as the generator was set to idle but even by the substandard diamond buying light, the size and the form of most of the diamonds was undeniable and from the center pile I spotted one that called out to me. It was marked by the emerald hue of a high quality stone, one of the first qualities Ygal had taught me to look for. I took the $20k out of the cheap vinyl bag and I set in on the table next to the parcels. I noticed him noticing that it was only about a fifth of the price of these three parcels, he drew breath to speak but I interjected, "I've brought this as a show of good faith. I couldn't be sure of the quality of the stones or the trustworthiness of a stranger so this is what I've brought." His eyes caught fire in what I now recognize must be the same frustration that a leopard just missing his prey is inflamed with.

"Why do you disrespect me?" he asked.

I didn't answer him, instead I took a cigarette and lighter from the bag. I lit the cigarette and rested my head back against the open window. I closed my eyes and began to think. He had never stated a figure verbally but I could tell by his demeanor that he was pricing these diamonds at the same rate I would be charged at the local jewelry store—retail full markup for the Western world.

I had just placed a small fortune right within his grasp and his reaction was a barely restrained threat. I took a deep drag of the cigarette and exhaled. The only reason he could be responding like this was that Harry had told him I would have five times this amount on me. Undoubtedly, never having seen a brick of US currency, he had estimated it at least twice its value, and now these guys were convinced that I was holding out on them. The man in front of me would not be satisfied with a morsel, he wanted everything I had or at least everything he thought I had. In reality, I had only a few thousand more. Now, without doubt, he knew I would expect to leave probably with all his diamonds and that I might not return. He was right about my intentions with that last part. A sure way to hedge against that risk would be to kill me, and then intimidate Harry for clues to the whereabouts of the non-existent rest of the cash. I was ashing my cigarette out of the open window behind me and had still not opened my eyes. My only logical play was to use their greed as my life support system, let them keep the twenty grand, use the valuable misinformation Harry had given them, feign like I had much more, leave with a fraction of the parcel's value but still with more diamond value than I'm leaving here, and convince them that I would trot right back here with all the money I had brought to their country and let them fleece me before my inevitable slaughter. Even after I decided that that was my plan, I kept my eyes closed and smoked that cigarette down to its butt. Part of my method of keeping calm was by finding ways to make this a performance and gamify it as much as possible. At last, I stood up to put my cigarette butt out of the window and to take a quick glance at the street to check on Harry. To my mortification, Harry's car was gone, the street was barren and silent, and my heart sank in my chest.

That's the most vulnerable I've ever felt in my life and it's because it's the most vulnerable position you could find yourself in. No one knew where I was, Shirley didn't know—she hadn't even seen me leave with Harry. I could literally be killed and left in this very spot to decompose and no one would be the wiser and no one would really care. I had to make it believable, he had to believe I would be back with a sizable sum that would tempt him to let me leave with a stone.

"Why you treat me with such disrespect?" menace oozed out of every syllable as he repeated the question.

I turned to speak to him, and replied, "I've treated you with every bit the same respect you've shown me."

The guards behind him moved to aim their weapons at me but their leader held up his hand, intuiting that I was about to make an offer. His mind had not left the thousands more that Harry had told him of, and I started to tug on that line of thinking like it was a life line.

"Look, I think we've had a little bit of a misunderstanding. I really didn't expect such a choice selection. I've got more money back in the safe at the hotel. I'll need a night manager to let me access it, but no problem. Let me take a sample back to show my partner why I'm spending everything we have. Maybe that one," I said, pointing with my chin toward the verdant precious stone, like I was just noticing it.

"I'll leave this here with you as a down payment on all three parcels," I added, giving the stacks of cash a pat. "And I'll take that rock there as proof for my partner. Surely it's worth only half of what I'm leaving."

His mood seemed to lighten ever so slightly, and we began to haggle over the price of all three parcels. Out of my bag, I pulled the Rappaport sheet. It's the blue book of the diamond market, and it's supposed to tell you the current average market price for different quality stones. But as far as I could tell, it was useless, and even if it wasn't, this one had been printed over a week ago back home. But at least it gave him a reason as to why I might be at a certain number. It was just something I could use as a focal point to make my argument believable.

We agreed to a price that I would not have agreed to if I were actually planning to return but I just wanted to get out of there with the one amazing stone that I really believed would be a good buy. It was at about this time that a fourth man appeared. He was dressed in the same fashion as the diamond dealer. However, his is a face I won't ever forget. This man was unable to hide his contempt for Americans, especially white ones. I don't know where he had been but obviously he had been listening to our conversation. He whispered something to the dealer, who looked at me and said, "This man will accompany you back to your hotel along with one of my men who will be driving."

He motioned behind him for one of his henchmen to come forth like he was calling a dog. I was still pretending to not know that Harry was gone, and I replied, "That's not necessary. I have Harry downstairs."

"Harry had an urgent matter to attend to and had to leave," the man said.

The lie was obvious but the robed diamond dealer spoke it as easily as he had spoken anything he'd said all night but I went along and agreed to accept their ride back to my hotel.

The new man insisted I ride up front and he sat directly behind me. The man with the gun put his rifle on the seat next to the new guy, and he drove. During the trip I turned around several times to speak to the man, and more than once, I caught him glaring. He avoided any small talk I was trying to make and rejected my offers of a cigarette. I kept on playing the part of the obtuse American but his hatred and distaste was impossible to miss. If I had to guess which one of these men was supposed to be the one that killed me, it would be the guy in the back seat. So after what seemed like an eternity and a really tense ride, we turned onto a road I recognized. We were now near the hotels. I remembered the other hotel that was just up the beach from the Mammy Yoko and I directed the driver there. Fortunately, they were not allowed to enter the compound. I wish I knew why but I don't. I got out at the guard gate telling the two men I would be right back and I gave the two guards in the guardhouse a friendly and somewhat loud hello, telling them it was nice to see them again. They had never seen me in their life but thinking I had to be a guest they responded politely. I took one last look at the guy in the back seat to say I'd be right back and there was the glare. He nodded his head. I walked into the new hotel lobby like I owned the place and no one doubted me for a minute; why would they? They could easily tell I wasn't from around these parts. My level of joy began to rise as I made my way through the lobby and out onto the back pool and beach area. I had checked this place out and was glad I had as I passed the monkey chained to the tree, my step quickened as I hit more familiar territory, and soon I was running down the sidewalk. I don't know why I noticed the noise of my boots on the sidewalk but I was uplifted by the cadence of concrete and leather as I ran up the back street away from an alternate course of events that would wind up with me dead within the hour. I came upon the back beach entrance to the Mammy Yoko hotel, and I knew I was home free. I had a big smile on my face thinking about the little escape act I had just pulled. I had just prevailed in the first real game of cat and mouse in Sierra Leone, and it wouldn't be the last.

Shirley looked like a nervous wreck when I entered the room, perched at the edge of the hotel bed. I asked her if she had seen Harry. A brief look of confusion crumpled her normally soft features and she replied, "I thought he was with you." I told her I had been but he had disappeared.

"Why would he do that?" Shirley asked.

I shrugged, "I don't know but you'd think he'd want his other five hundred."

I can't know for sure if Harry was threatened once I was upstairs, or if he'd been part of the plan to part me with my money from the beginning. But I didn't want to stick around to find out. I knew all I needed to know now. Yes, there were diamonds to be had here, but now I knew you had to go up-country. In town, if you were lucky enough to find a dealer who was not going to rob you, they were still charging very high prices, perhaps in some sort of an attempt to compensate for past losses. But it was clear to me now that the men that were selling in town were not the men that were digging them up.

Under the incandescent lights of the room, the stone was even more beautiful. At half the size of the others in the parcels I had seen, this diamond shone twice as brightly as its counterparts. Shirley let out a slow wow when she saw it, and I was happy when she asked if it was fluorescing. "It's an illusion, I think." I told her how Ygal had specified a certain characteristic to be on the lookout for, and literally on the first viewing of Sierra Leone diamonds, I had spotted one.

Getting the stone on the plane was easy. It was small but just in case we were searched, we had to hide it. It was illegal not to declare any instrument including diamonds and cash in excess of $10k. So Shirley put the stone in a plastic tampon applicator and off we went. The flight back to Holland was not without its bit of drama. I was starting to see that Shirley was prone to little "freak outs," for lack of a better description. She was a good soul and a great person but perhaps not suited for what we had planned. Suddenly, it struck her that she could get something known as toxic shock syndrome from keeping the plastic in her for too long of a period of time.

At this point, I was sure we were free and clear, and we wouldn't be looked at very closely at customs. They passed the declaration forms through-out the cabin as we were nearing our destination. And just like on the way in, I declared nothing. Shirley had gone to the bathroom halfway through our first flight back and the diamond was now in my pocket.

For the flight between Amsterdam and Atlanta, Shirley and I didn't speak much. We were still in business class and it was really good to have food and drink that you not only liked but that you completely trusted. Still we both wanted this trip to be over. It had only been a week but what a week! We arrived at Miami International, where Shirley's white firebird had been parked in the long-term lot. We put our bags in the trunk and she drove home. She dropped me off at home and we said our goodbyes. She said she wanted to go home and rest, and tomorrow, she would have her hand looked at. I told her I would make the insurance claim in the morning as well and I did.

Crossing the threshold into the cool darkness of the Kendall apartment was a return to my sanctuary, and the sight of the maps of Sierra Leone strewn across my bed and earmarked books still peppered about the living room filled with me a profound satisfaction only surpassed by the excitement that surged through me when I held the fluorescing diamond up in the light.

CHAPTER 3

I couldn't wait to see what Ygal would have to say about the diamond. I didn't have to wait long. The first thing the next morning I called and asked if I could visit. "Of course," was his answer.

It was another beautiful South Florida day and it felt like life in general held a lot of promise.

I was buzzed into his office, where he had already been hard at work on the grinding wheel evidenced by the fine diamond powder that coated anything near his work station. I had put the stone in a bandanna, which I was presently unfolded at his desk. He walked over from the wheel and looked down wearing an expression of disbelief and said, "Get the hell out of here, you found this?"

"Yes," I affirmed, with a bit of pride. He sat down and took out his jeweler's loupe and began to examine it. He put the stone back down on the desk, and looked up at me, "This has got to be the greatest case of beginner's luck I have ever seen. Or maybe it was meant to be—who knows. But if all goes well, this diamond could end up being a 4 carat flawless D. at 10 to 11 thousand per carat wholesale. But who knows, the retail price could fetch three times that."

His voice began to speed up a little with excitement as he continued to explain that back in the day a one carat D flawless used to fetch as much as 70 thousand dollars a carat in retail settings.

He said he had cleaved stones before, but that he didn't want to take a chance on cleaving this one as one false move could shatter the stone, rendering it worthless. However, he had a man in the New York diamond district that did nothing but cleave. He would insure the stone and send it by mail to his colleague.

I had begun planning my next trip. I had all the proof of concept I needed and I knew the most important place, what the locals called the "up-country" was still unseen. I was determined to go back and find my way there. I don't think the wildlife photographer back story had even been necessary. But what was necessary was going to be someone reliable to watch my back. Someone I could trust.

I was back to practice and hanging out with friends that would come watch us rehearse, we had hope and pretty soon we would have the money from the diamond to keep the studio going and possibly enough to fund another trip.

Eli had introduced me to an interesting fellow by the name of Gigi. He was an Italian guy but he studied in France. When he spoke, it was with a thick French accent—a mixture really of French and Italian. He had taught himself English on the fly and had an impressive grasp of the language for someone who arrived in the United States without knowing a word. He wasn't very tall but he looked like an MMA fighter with shoulder-length, brown hair and hazel eyes. His arms were covered with scars doubtlessly acquired while wrestling with unruly metals working his job as a foreman in a scrap recycling facility. A job he negotiated for himself on a trial basis while still learning English. His work ethic and tenacity rapidly propelled him into a leadership role.

All in all, I was impressed with Gigi. He coupled the most charming aspects of European sensibilities and worldliness with an all-American work ethic, a portion of which I think was imparted to him by the great American propaganda machine Hollywood, but whether *The Terminator* or *Rambo* had anything to do with how he comported himself, he embodied a little bit of that bad-assery regardless. One episode stands out above the rest. Early on, when I had just decided that Gigi might be a good candidate to travel into the jungles of Sierra Leone with, we set up a lunch time meeting at his workplace.

I got to the scrapyard to be faced with a not so uncommon attempted theft. A local crackhead was trying to steal scrap from the yard to sell back to the yard. I got out of the green bug and watched as the thief armed with a knife was keeping a half dozen guys away by slicing wildly through the air. Gigi walked calmly between the befuddled pack of men and approached the thief. He had a cigarette dangling out of his mouth and the thief was much taller than he was. The thief squared up with the approaching challenger and delivered a wild backhanded swing of the knife aimed at Gigi's chest, with the combative economy of motion typically only displayed by a Judoka, Gigi caught the attacker's knife hand in a supinated grip and then twisted it backwards in practically the same movement, at once defending himself and immobilizing his assailant. The knife clattered over the concrete and the thief subsequently plunged to his knees, at which point Gigi simply let him go. As he began to walk away, the half dozen men who had been trying to get the guy suddenly rushed him and set about to beating him, I know it sounds bad, but it was almost comical, as Gigi turned to yell at the men "Oh, now you are going to beat him up!?"

"Get back to work. Let him go. We can't even call the police now he will sue us, get your asses back to work!"

I knew right there and then that that was my guy. If he wasn't interested, I would have to simply sell it to him till I convinced him it was something I was good at. But fortunately one of the first things Gigi said after hearing me out was, "I have some vacation time saved up." I knew he was game.

So, in Miami, rehearsals were going as usual, Gigi would call me every night after rehearsal and we spent hours making our plans on the phone. We were discussing some details about the last trip and how Shirley's hand did end up requiring surgery to reset the bone. Luckily the insurance we had purchased paid the claim. Gigi and I were in the midst of one of these conversations when the events unfolding on my tiny television screen once again caught my eyes. The news had cut to a crime scene and in big, white letters, the caption, "Brazen daylight diamond heist" was rolling across the bottom of the screen. I turned up the volume to hear the broadcaster reporting that the Seybold building had been robbed, more specifically it was a mail truck picking up packages from the Seybold building.

It startled us for a moment to think that the stone Shirley and I had brought back could have been stolen, but then we thought, what are the chances? Still it was on my mind so I called Ygal first thing the next morning, and that's when I got the news that sure enough our diamond had been aboard that truck on its way to New York when it was robbed at gunpoint.

Ygal said it was a shame but that he had insured the stone for the most he could get for a rough stone that had not yet been cut or polished. The insurance claim was for $30k, which Ygal paid me for in advance of the settlement. When I asked him why he would do that, he responded that he felt it was his responsibility as the stone had been left in his care. I'll never know what became of my first diamond but I do know that $10k profit was not enough to risk my life for.

It all felt a little too convenient to be coincidence. The final value of that cleaved stone was unclear but the fact that it was untraceable and had zero previous documentation had its obvious benefits. Either way there was mystery in the mix right out of the gate.

I was already able to relate several certainties about our next trip to Gigi, for instance we would not be staying in Freetown, we would be venturing into the up-country, which was essentially the jungle proper. Tribal people inhabited those lands, and we would need to pack accordingly—there were no 7-11s in the bush. Allying ourselves with a guide would be of seminal importance, and we needed more of that all-important life-blood in business: money.

The sudden disappearance of my stone illustrated a sardonic irony of all business—the margins always seem to shrink somewhere. The Red Hot Chili Peppers lyrics spring to mind, *"Wait a minute, lost it at the city limit, say goodbye, cause they will find a way to trim it."* I had out maneuvered the treacheries of the actual jungle only to have the concrete jungle ultimately claim the lion's share, and again we found ourselves plotting how to tiptoe across the Atlantic on a shoestring budget.

Both of our jobs just paid enough to pay the month to month bills. I had worked as a painter, a local stagehand, I was a trailer salesman, a bartender, a phone sales rep. I was cleaning boat bottoms. Breathing through a hookah, I would go in the water and scrape boat bottoms 8 hours a day. I have never been lazy and I've burnt the candle at both ends in order to succeed. I could just never shake the feeling that valuable time was being wasted and there was somewhere else I was supposed to be. In my mind that somewhere else was on the road with my band. So I may have been at the point where I would have done anything to get the money that might help me fund this dream. I just had to feel that I had done everything humanly possible to make that dream come true. There are so many people who try to convince you that you should settle, that you should accept what they accept and be grateful. And I respect having gratitude but a prime example of what I did not want to become was an uncle of mine that I lived with for a while in Miami. Uncle Fred, he worked for forty years in a factory that made zippers—forty years at the same position. He took a small pension when he retired, just enough to barely make ends meet. His wife had died of cancer about halfway through his tenure in zipper hell, so he was a widower now, and that was the end of his story. He was one of the people in my life who championed that sentiment of what I would come to describe as the "worker bee mentality"—gratefulness for what little could be acquired that way included. And that was always my biggest fear, that I would be that person. I had to prove to myself that I could break free of what I considered to be a common cultural delusion.

So when the opportunity presented itself, I did not pass it up. FarrCry had played a show at a Ft. Lauderdale club called City Limits, where I met a Colombian guy, who had come to our show with a neighbor friend, a girl I had met at the pool at our apartment complex. He was a very boisterous type and wanted to make sure everyone knew he was related to a well known cartel boss. I'm not going to say which boss because I'm not sure I believe him but he had come to the complex in a brand new Ferrari, and a few days later, I had seen him with the neighbor in a new Porsche. But for all I know, he worked for an exotic car dealership.

In doing my level best for the band, I would field each and every offer. And now it was this guy saying he had an offer for the band. He sent the neighbor girl over to my apartment one afternoon to invite me to some club or another to discuss this offer. I don't remember the club other than it was in Coral Gables and it was a dance club. Not the sort of place I frequented. The champagne was flowing and there was no shortage of trips to the bathroom by either guys or girls. There wasn't any plan at all. I could tell this guy was just putting on airs for anyone who would listen. I had been sober for over two years and I wasn't even tempted, as the night dragged on though, I was becoming a bit irritated with the boisterous behavior and ridiculous claims of wealth and status within the cartel.

The concealed weapons were being flashed now for some sort of clout and the talk was becoming more and more dangerous. I couldn't wait for the night to end so I could leave and never speak to this person again. I had been drinking water and looking for my reason to escape this little nightmare I had walked into. When the guy turned to me and speaking close enough for me to smell his breath—a mixture of alcohol, cigarettes and funk mouth—he said I should get the next couple of rounds of champagne. And by round, he meant bottle at about $250 a pop in the private section we were seated in.

We had come to the club from the apartment complex together in a brand new Lincoln, but his Ferrari was parked in the parking spot belonging to the neighbor girl back home at the Courts of Kendall. The valet had the keys to the Lincoln but I had spotted the unmistakable shape of the Ferrari key in the neighbor girl's purse, which was now partially open and visible on the table in front of her. My anger was sort of rising. How did this obtuse idiot not realize that you don't invite a practically starving artist to an expensive club, and once you are six bottles in, ask him to pay. Two bottles was a month's rent at the time. Never mind that the majority of my meals were purchased at a 7-11 gas station on Kendall and 148th street with the very credit card I was now being pressured to use to buy bottles of grossly overpriced champagne! It was more than my sensibilities could tolerate.

You don't manage a huge scrapyard in Miami without getting to know some people. And for better or worse, that was the case with Gigi. Scrap came from all sorts of places. Junkies would steal scrap metal to sell at these recyclers, house remodelers, can collectors, demolition companies, the list goes on and on. Scrap metal is big business and the occasional chop shop would donate their scrap just to destroy evidence. It wasn't like it was a daily thing but chop shops and scrap yards are sometimes closely related.

If you carried a cell phone back in the day it was a conspicuous pocket whale they were big and bulky and the people who were now acquiring them tended to speak loudly. I didn't have one of those, but payphones were still everywhere. I ordered the first bottle of champagne and as the neighbor girl and the cartel wannabe went for a dance I took the Ferrari key. By the time the bottle arrived, they were returning from the dance floor and the waitress poured them each a glass. My glass was turned upside down in front of me and the waitress knew I had not been drinking. She set a glass of water in front of me and offered a nice smile. I excused myself with a joke about the water going through me like water, but it wasn't just a joke; I was also trying to make a point. They didn't seem to get it. I went to the phone and called Gigi, I apprised him of my current situation and of my plan and location, I asked him to make a quick call regarding anyone's need for a brand new Ferrari. I went back to the table where the bottle of champagne was already empty. He was loudly sniffing at the table, and the girl and her purse were both gone. This fact made me slightly nervous as her missing key was still in my pocket. But she returned sniffing loudly as well, and seemingly without a clue about the missing key.

I ordered a second bottle of champagne—this one may have lasted 20 minutes.

Gigi had made the call and help was on the way. Two gentlemen driving a hot-rodded old truck that had been restored and customized would be outside shortly. I was to just hand them the key. We were now on the third bottle; it took a total of five, but on my subsequent trip outside after ordering the fifth bottle of champagne over $1300 that night, the boys in the truck had pulled up and with barely a word between us, I handed off the key with a handshake.

I don't know how much time we missed them by as we left the club less than an hour after that last bottle. But I was the designated driver and the two of them were drunk and yapping away the whole way home. I felt fortunate that Mr. Cartel had let me take the keys to his Lincoln after a little bit of insistence from the valet that he was in no shape to drive.

When we got home, they went right to her apartment without even noticing the missing Ferrari.

I laughed a little maniacal but truly satisfying laugh as my key hit my lock.

I woke up at eleven the next morning to see a police car where the Ferrari once was. They were both out there in the same clothes that they had on when we got home last night. They hadn't been to sleep, and they were not making a good impression on the police from the looks of it. I laughed again.

After a quick cup of coffee and a bagel, I headed over to see Gigi. There was a little Cuban restaurant, a lunch spot really, just about a block away from the scrapyard where we used to meet. We would get a colada and talk about our plans. This particular day was memorable because as I took my seat, Gigi casually slid an unassuming plain brown paper bag across the little outdoor table, presumably filled with napkins or something.

"Be careful with that. They paid us $75'000," he said, after a bite of the *ropa vieja* he had ordered for lunch.

I was pleasantly surprised and asked, "I thought the going rate was 50?"

"The extra is in consideration for past favors rendered."

We continued to pull off small schemes and secured a few small loans and even after travel expenses were accounted for, it looked like we had safely squirreled away about $100,000 between the Ferrari heist, our other efforts, and the insurance payout for the stone.

Finally, the time to depart and try our hand against fate had arrived again, we had decided to stick with KLM Airlines but this time, our flight would take us through London instead of Amsterdam, and we would have to take a shuttle between Heathrow and Gatwick airports. Once again the KLM business class flight was really superb. I can't imagine how much more they could possibly be doing for you in first class that they weren't already doing in business class. Gigi was a very good sport about my no drinking rule. I had even more respect for him when they served some liquor on the flight that he had not seen since leaving Europe to live in the States, but still he respected the rule. I was impressed.

Taking the shuttle on that day between Gatwick and Heathrow was the first time I had ever seen any part of London. I don't know what I was expecting, I had always pictured it as a cold, rainy, gray place. But this was as beautiful a spring day as I've ever seen in the tropics. It hadn't really occurred to me that we would have to pass through customs again. We had, of course, not claimed the currency we were bringing in, and it was currently in that same money belt that I had used on my last trip with Shirley. I also had a brick in each boot. Gigi was carrying a couple of bricks, all of it undeclared. When the customs officer asked if I had anything to declare, I said no. But for some reason, he decided to have me open my duffle bag, which I did of course. And then when he said he was going to pat me down, I became concerned pretty quickly. I began to tell him some knock-knock joke I had heard recently. His hands struck all the usual places people smuggle things. I timed the joke so that just as he put his hand directly on the money belt, I was delivering the punch line. Even though he hadn't given any outward impression that he was amused by my impromptu comedy, however he did chuckle, so he was listening, and I did my best to look the part of the carefree American traveler. Gigi was waved right through customs and stood waiting and watching for me maybe twenty feet away.

Always a great one for mixing metaphors, in his thick Italian accent, Gigi said to me, "You were cool like a cucumber."

I exclaimed under my breath, "He put his hand right on it!"

I was in total shock that our plans had not imploded right then and there.

"I know—that's why I just said what I said," Gigi retorted.

We chuckled and kept walking towards our gate. We arrived in Lungi on a Thursday. We had fourteen days from the time we hit the tarmac to pull something off, and the clock was ticking. The mysteries of the upcountry awaited.

CHAPTER 4

The flight arrived at about the same time of day as it had on the last trip, but this time, we decided to take a helicopter to Freetown. The previous year, the company that ran the tours and airport trips had had three helicopters in their fleet, but since then, one had crashed into the bay taking the same route we were about to take. There had been a number of deaths involved, but also a few passengers had survived. It didn't exactly inspire confidence, and to be honest, I never liked helicopters. It is the only flying machine that to me appears to be fighting against itself with its two-propeller design. Thankfully, we had an uneventful crossing. The helipad was situated between the two main hotels on the beach. We were once again staying at the Mammy Yoko. It was a very short shuttle ride to the front gate of the hotel and the shuttle dropped us off inside the hotel compound right in front of the lobby.

We checked in without incident. We were sharing a room, and we just wanted to put our bags down and go have a look around. It was dark already but the beach bar was buzzing with activity as was the street in front of the hotel.

As we headed out the back way towards the ocean, we stepped out onto the sidewalk, and as we began heading towards the bar, a group of young guys came towards us. And as would have been the case in certain places in Miami, we began to cross the street to avoid them. But it was Gigi who stopped and said, "We're not in Miami—why are we crossing the street?"

And so, instead, we continued towards the group. I said before that this was a place of contrasts. The young men were very nice and welcoming as well as very expressive and interested in meeting us. It was impossible to believe that these young men would soon probably be involved in the Revolutionary United Front (RUF). After 17 years of political stability, the new generation was coming of age, and in a few months, the world would once again see just how brutal a 15year-old boy could be. We continued on to the beach bar, where I saw a familiar face or two from the last trip. We said hello to a few people, had some hummus and flatbread, and a couple of cokes. We asked the bartender if perhaps he knew of a guide—someone with a car we could hire. I suspected I would see Pauline back at the hotel in the morning, when the tours office opened. But I wasn't too sure of what I would say to her. I thought it best to wait and see what her reaction to seeing me was going to be. We told the bartender which hotel we were staying at, and we headed back to get some sleep.

It was a beautiful start to the day on that Friday morning. Looking out at the Atlantic Ocean, which seemed so desolate from this coast, made you wonder about what was possible and why certain things weren't already there.

Gigi and I were each in our respective beds in the hotel room, when Gigi started to wonder how good the protection offered by the stun guns we would be carrying would be.

As he sat there smoking a cigarette and contemplating this important question, I saw the idea come across his face, and asked, "You aren't thinking what I think you're thinking, are you?"

He laughed, and stuck the stun gun to his left thigh and pulled the trigger. Almost instantly, his body went rigid and made an attempt to bow backwards. I wondered why he didn't just let it go because he was starting to turn purple and was spitting into the air. The cigarette he had been smoking was now burning the bed. That's when I realized, he couldn't let it go. His grip was locked shut with a heavy duty muscle contraction he could not control. I had to strike his arm with my foot from the other bed. I kicked him and he dropped it and after a moment's recovery, he glanced up and matter of factly remarked, "Thanks, it works."

We looked at each other for a second longer with eyes wide, and suddenly, we both burst out laughing. That had been a lesson, and now we knew how hilarious it could be to almost electrocute yourself. Our laughter was interrupted by the telephone ringing.

The speaker on the other end inquired, "Mr. Mark?"

To which I responded, "Yes."

It was a man by the name of Mohamed on the line. The bartender at the beach bar had given him and his partner, Nelson, my name and hotel.

Gigi and I went down to meet them. We discussed wanting to go up-country and needing guides. Nelson was a man of maybe 25. He was slight and wore a beard. He was a soft-spoken guy, and seemed a bit shy at first, glancing down often when being spoken to. Mohamed was a tall African and very much the salesman—he was outgoing and very respectful. They were driving an old Mercedes sedan; it had seen better days but it was still a Mercedes.

Before going to the up-country, we had decided to go north to Kabala for one day. We were only on day two and had 13 days left before our flight, and Gigi had been doing some research of his own and there had been gold mining outfits in the mid 80s that had said in a magazine interview that even though the Russians had mined there for all it was worth, there were still deposits there. We would leave at sunrise the next morning.

That Saturday came fast. I didn't sleep much that night. This was getting real, and we would be traveling with a lot of cash. We planned to leave half of our money in the hotel's safety deposit box, but would still carry somewhere in the neighborhood of 50k. Nelson and Mohamed met us downstairs. We had a duffle bag with bottled water and about ten pounds of trail mix. Not the kind with the chocolate. The sun was just ascending over the horizon as we packed into the old Mercedes and struck out for Kabala.

Gigi had always had a love of cars and motorcycles, a passion I shared to a much lesser degree. In addition to the hot-rod Chevy, he had enjoyed a factory sponsorship from Suzuki motocross motorcycles, and just generally liked to drive fast. So it was no surprise when he asked Mohamed if he could take the wheel. The road we were traveling on was red smooth clay often contrasted with deep green and shadowed jungles or tall brown sawgrass at its sides. It appeared to go on forever. Behind us, we were leaving a huge maroon dust cloud as the old Benz pushed 80mph. Mohamed became a little concerned and said this wasn't exactly his car, it belonged to his brother-in-law, who had only lent it to him so he could do this job. Gigi pushed the car to about 90mph and yelled at Mohamed from the driver's seat, "If I break it, I'll buy it!"

Normally on such a serious trip so far from a hospital with so much cash, I would not have liked the idea of racing through Africa, but I knew Gigi could drive. To be honest, he looked like he was having the absolute time of his life. We reached Kabala about two hours ahead of schedule.

As we neared the town of Kabala, we passed the first of three checkpoints we would encounter on that road. Checkpoints are a funny thing in Africa. I suppose they serve a greater purpose but to us they were just "shake down" points. The way it usually went was our driver would get out and talk to the guards at the checkpoint, and sometimes they would come and ask to see papers. They might check your trunk and or your luggage but they usually didn't put their hands on you. And 40 or 50 leones per person in the vehicle seemed to be doing the trick. But as we approached the third and last checkpoint before entering the town, we couldn't see anyone there. It appeared to be empty, and we slowed to a crawl as we all looked left and right but no one was visible to us. Mohamed, who was still in the back seat, said, "Well, just go then. What can be done?"

The town was in sight, and we could see people, so we continued. We drove around a turnabout, and before we knew what was happening, we were surrounded by several Toyota-style pickup trucks, and there were a few men in the back of each truck. They began yelling at us to exit the car and they had rifles in hand. The four of us exited the car and they had us stand there while one of them spoke into a radio. A voice crackled over the radio that the constable was on his way. I started to ask Mohamed what that meant but was immediately shouted down, "No speaking!"

I knew Gigi and I had to look worried but what made it really unsettling was the look on Mohamed's face. This evidently was not standard operating procedure.

A small crowd from the very edge of town had gathered around us, and they parted as if to let someone through. Obviously, this was the constable. He was a tall man, and he wore gray slacks and a black guayabera-style shirt. The first thing he did was demand our passports, which Gigi and I nervously surrendered to him. He was seemingly at least very angry about Gigi having been seen by the guards ignoring the checkpoint, which isn't how we remembered it.

He was a much taller man than either one of us, and he approached me and leaned in closely, very closely, mere inches from my face. Looking intently into my eyes, he spoke slowly and deliberately, "What is your mission?"

This man had an intimidating aura. If you've ever seen a picture of Haiti's dictatorial Papa Doc, that was the cloth this man was cut from, only he was much taller. His accent was unfamiliar to me, even with my newly forming familiarity with West African dialects. I was distinctly bothered by his choice of words and the calculated cadence he spoke with. I wanted to make it clear quickly that I was much closer to an entrepreneurial tourist than any type of government operative for a foreign power. Some of the men who had stopped us initially still stood with weapons half-trained on our group.

Speaking a little faster than I normally do, I explained that we were only in Kabala to purchase snakeskin. I had seen hides in Freetown but I was told that here in this region is where the best pelts ophidian or otherwise were to be found.

He squinted increasingly stormy eyes at me as I finished speaking. Then the constable regarded us with obvious contempt for a moment before practically spitting out each word individually in his thick accent, "You expect me to believe a big bad American has come here" —he made a dramatic slow gesture towards the encroaching palm jungle and the looming checkpoint soldiers as if to emphasize his next point—"All the way into the heart of Africa, for the skin of A SNAKE!"

I was surprised at the sudden outburst and the decibels he had summoned. He had put away all pretensions of a calm demeanor. We had clearly insulted his intelligence with our fib. Like any professional grifter, I insisted that indeed that was why we had come. He ignored my response and told us to follow the men to the jail until he could decide what to do. Running a check-point was a very serious matter. I couldn't tell if all this emotion was a ruse or if he was being completely serious but there were automatic weapons pointed at us, the whole town had seen us pass the checkpoint and this man now held our passports.

Still I was sort of stuck on his choice of words "big bad American," especially given the size difference between us. This was beginning to get serious, and I was afraid this guy might actually detain us. So I did the only thing I could think of. I began to bribe him right there in front of God and everyone. I asked with all the sincerity I could muster, "Isn't it possible to perhaps pay a fine instead of going to jail?"

I had learned my lesson about keeping separate cash so as not to reveal myself like I had that night at the airport on the first trip.

We had also learned that it was possible to exchange American dollars for the national fiat at the hotel, which we had already done, so we were carrying a very small sum of leones as well. And our money was separated accord-ingly. I had not been completely intimidated out of my wits, so I decided we would start with Sierra Leone money. I pulled out that particular roll which contained about 500 leones the equivalent of about $50 US.

He said that would only pay for the fine. There was also a cost for bond-ing out of jail and coming back for a court date. I couldn't believe my ears—this guy was dead serious. I told him that's all the money that I had.

Gigi then reached in his pocket and produced a fifty dollar bill. The constable seemed suddenly much less angry. He took the fifty from Gigi and put it in his shirt. He turned to one of the men with him and handed him the 500 leones with some instruction spoken in a different dialect. He waved off the men and took our passports out of his pocket. He handed them back to us and we each breathed a heavy sigh of relief. He instructed us to make our way to the constable's office and register with the police. We agreed and he pointed us in the direction. We began to walk that way. I'm guessing the fifty was already burning a hole in his pocket because he left with his driver in a different direction. We were standing there now, just the four of us alone and saying to each other, what the hell just almost happened?

There were still a few people watching us, but by and large, most had lost interest. It was only then that I took a look at the town. It was a busy place, a Muslim community, a sort of melting pot of Africans, Egyptians, Liberians. We decided to interpret his direction as more of a directive we should follow if we decided to stay the night in his town. We did not, we got quickly back in the car with Mohamed at the wheel and we began driving out of town, again we could see no one at the checkpoint as we approached. Gigi and I looked once at each other and then towards Mohamed and with our voices full of the thrill of escape, we exclaimed, "Punch it!"

Poor Mohamed jumped in surprise at our revelous cry, and confusedly asked, "Punch what?"

Nelson finally spoke up, "It's an American movie thing. It means drive fast brother!"

Mohamed put the pedal to the metal and as the sun hovered low in the sky, we pressed deep tire treads into the flat paths back to Freetown, the tall sawgrass on either side of the road swaying with the momentum of our passing. In retrospect, although things had gone almost completely wrong from a purely gold and diamond expedition point of view, I was nonetheless glad we had decided to go to Kabala. We had learned a very valuable lesson.

CHAPTER 5

We returned to Freetown and the Mammy Yoko hotel well after nightfall. We asked Mohamed to be back at first light again and he agreed. We had trail mix accompanied by room temperature water for dinner, as the hotel kitchen was closed for the night

We got up before sunrise and lit a couple of cigarettes. We were both starving at this point, so we decided to see what the restaurant had to offer if and when it opened. Fuel had become increasingly hard to get in Freetown, and as a result, many deliveries were being delayed and supplies interrupted. The office Pauline had occupied sat empty. On this particular day, the restaurant had fresh eggs and we were able to get some scrambled eggs and flatbread. First light had come, and I spotted Mohamed just outside of the compound. I walked to the lobby door and signaled to him with a hand gesture saying we would take 5 minutes. We returned quickly back to the room to grab the duffle bag with the bottled water, and Gigi took his quinine and reminded me to do the same. I agreed but I didn't really take it. I thought it had been making me a little nauseated yesterday and decided to skip it today.

At breakfast, Gigi and I had discussed hiring more help. We needed someone with a little clout, we needed a slightly bigger fish that we could feed once and it would protect us from all the little fish we kept having to pay off. Mohamed had come alone on this day, saying Nelson had a family matter to attend to. We had been paying Mohamed and Nelson on a day to day basis so far. Yesterday Nelson had received $80 for his services. We told Mohamed that perhaps it was just as well. We wanted to approach a uniformed police officer—one with a gun preferably, and attempt to hire him to escort us past the checkpoints we were sure to encounter. Mohamed totally agreed with the idea, and we began heading towards the police station.

On our way to the station, we saw a truck with some military personnel. They were the government army. They wore khaki uniforms with brown helmets and carried Russian-made rifles. They were loading up to go towards the border with Liberia, where there was word of a mass migration into Sierra Leone from Prince Johnson's Liberia. The word was that atrocities were being inflicted on his own citizens in some bizarre display of power. These men would assist refugees and prevent any war crimes from occurring within Sierra Leone. Also in town, which was really bustling by now, were the blue hats. They were an international peacekeeping unit sponsored by the UN.

As we watched the men load into the transport, we spotted a soldier who was giving orders to the men. He had captain's bars and a red beret, he wore large mirrored sunglasses and his uniform was regulation neat and clean.

As I approached, I took the liberty of calling him by rank. "Excuse me, captain, good morning. Would it be possible to speak with you when you have a moment?"

He looked very serious and as if he was about to chastise me for interrupting his order giving. But slowly a smile crossed his lips, and he said, "American right?"

I was very proud that I had been right about the two gold bars on his shirt lapels. I tried to make my response sound halfway military, "Yes sir. Allow me to introduce myself. Mark Christian is my name. This man is our driver Mohamed, and this is my partner Gigi. We simply wanted to inquire if for a fee, of course, you could guide us past the checkpoints on the way upcountry."

He turned and walked towards the truck that his subordinates had been loading and from the cab he produced a gun belt. Holstered in it was an officer's sidearm. He strode back towards us as he fashioned the gun belt on his waist with a casual, business-like confidence and familiarity. "You are in luck. We are all going that way. My fee is $200."

He gave instructions to a man who wore a sergeant's patch on his arm, and we showed him our car. Mohamed had filled the gas tank at 3 am last night. Additionally, he had spent the night in the car to be first in line when fuel was resupplied to the station in the morning, and he had filled the spare cans in the trunk. Only then had he gone by his own home to shower and change clothes. He was scoring points with his punctuality and work ethic, and it was really good that his daily rate meant so much to him.

On the long drive up the mountainous terrain, the captain whom I now gauged to be about 35 years old was expounding on the situation in Liberia, twisting in the passenger seat to address us as sun beams danced across the opaque panes of his reflective aviators. He described horrific encounters with racial cleansing, looting and other massacres, and his increasingly unsuccessful attempts to keep that chaos from spilling over into Sierra Leone; both in terms of physical incursions and ideologically. Before falling into silence, the captain remarked, "The winds of change are coming, and it brings the vultures."

Going up-country was at once beautiful and frightening. Roads washed out frequently and became impassable. There could be precipitous drops on narrow switchbacks, crater-like potholes peppered the path where there was one. However, going through the checkpoints now with our driver and our army captain was a total breeze. He would simply wave them off and the barrier would be lifted.

We arrived at a village. Its entrance, just like Kabala, had a security gate and a checkpoint. Only this one had a sign prominently displayed that read, "No white man allowed beyond this point." We were beginning to encroach on diamond-rich ground, routinely soaked in blood by colonial invaders and warring tribes alike. A wave of the hand would not suffice to bring foreigners where they were forbidden. We had been honest with the captain on the way up about our desire to perhaps purchase diamonds here or do diamond business in some way. We didn't need much of a backstory as just being here with our driver and military escort was proof enough of our intentions, and any other reason but diamond hunting would have been a ludicrously transparent lie. We had already learned in Kabala both what crossing certain boundaries and a lie might cost us. I gave the captain another $100 to try to buy us a little goodwill. A few elder men all dressed in white and wearing sandals congregated and had a discussion, which took a little too long for comfort, and I thought we were being denied but eventually, the captain returned and informed me our token had been well-received.

I was once in Vegas and was watching as a crap table was ebbing and flowing, hot one moment with lots of excited action and people cheering a point to cold the next moment, when someone threw craps (which is a losing roll if you're not familiar with the game). The collective sigh of grief and deflation was palpable, as if the whole gathering had witnessed Lady Luck hike up her skirts and flee the room.

I knew I couldn't predict those hot and cold runs but I had a feeling that the casino men working the table probably had a feeling for the rhythm of these things. So my strategy was easy. I would take a seat directly to the right of the croupier. Every time I put a bet down for myself, I put one down for them and would, of course, indicate as much to the croupier with a hand gesture or a nod. After a few passes, a dealer would catch on and begin to speak out of the side of his mouth at me, "Pass." Or "Don't pass." This went on and in no time we had a hand signal pidgin language worked out. When dealers went on a break and were relieved, I continued my strategy with the replacement, and in no time, they also obliged. We sat there gaming that table all night, time moved in a blur and a stack of chips steadily piled up in front of me. I was exuberant to be beating the system. This must be what it feels like to have connections. The crowd is what signaled to me that morning had finally come through furtive glances at wrist watches, yawns, and bewildered looks directed into the crevices of now empty wallets. The spell of the gambling house was beginning to break as casino staff busily hurried off glasses, plates, and reset tables for the following evening's debauchery and illusions. On the way out, some of the dealers I had partnered with gave me discrete and sincere "Thank yous," which I returned in kind. My very first time at a craps table in Vegas, and I had made 3 grand, which meant that the dealers had made 3 grand. They, of course, had to split it five or six ways. But still, $500 extra for 6 guys just doing their shift—it had to feel pretty good to them too. That same concoction equal parts bribery, discretion, and humility, composed the formula that I was applying now in the up-country where the stakes were much higher.

The captain said we would be allowed to come into the village, and we idled in slowly over hilly terrain. The sign for no whites seemed to peer at me through the window. That was a bit of an odd feeling. There was a big shade tree just off the side of the road, and we parked there. The captain said he had to rejoin his men who should by now be in a nearby village. Mohamed knew where this village was, and we asked him to please drive the captain. It was still early in the day, and it was only a few kilometers each way. Gigi and I bid the captain farewell, and as we parted, he told us that he would leave our names at the checkpoints as they went back down to Freetown to pick up more men. That was a big relief, and a good sign that the captain had liked us, and was not against us coming up to buy rough.

Mohamed gave a big smile and a thumbs-up, as he remarked, "That is *craze* man, you are very lucky."

Mohamed and the captain had just departed, and we began heading deeper into the village. This wasn't like being in any town in the USA. There were no hotels, no restaurants, no convenience stores. So it felt as if there was no neutral place to be, and all eyes were very much upon us. We really didn't know where to go next but we didn't have to worry about that for too long. A small group of 4 or 5 men was heading down the middle of the red dust road right towards us. "Welcome," a young man greeted us from the forefront of the group. I noticed that his teeth were almost perfect. How was that even possible? He was not a big man, maybe 5'8", but he was compact, and looked to be mostly lean muscle. He spoke English with an emphasis on his enunciation, "My name is Alusaine. My father is the village chief."

He extended a hand, which I grasped and shook. Gigi quipped, "Well, then that makes you a prince, does it not?"

Alusaine's welcoming grin broadened into a bright smile. A few of the men accompanying him gave knowing glances at each other and let out little laughs, almost as if Gigi had hit on some inside joke. Obviously, this young man liked being the next in line for Chief.

We didn't really waste any time with more small talk, mostly because Alusaine was quickly getting to the point of his warm welcome and big smile. "While your escort was speaking with the elders, I was watching the two of you sitting in the car, and I had a very good feeling right away, that you two men were going to be bringing good business to my village. You could say I have been waiting for you but I didn't know it until I saw you."

"Come, come, let us show you around the village," he said. As we walked, the young prince told us how each home we were passing was built one at a time with the whole village pitching in, in one way or another. Diamond mining was how this village generated income for materials for building homes as well as stoves and pots and pans for cooking. The cooking appeared to be done outside, under partial cover. There was an iron stove set up over a fire pit in the center of the village.

Alusaine paused in front of the door of one of the nicer dwellings, and said, "This one belongs to me. Come in let me show you."

The home was made of wood with a thatched roof; the floor was bare dirt floor but almost perfectly flat, and funny as it may sound, it looked swept. The rooms had windows but no glass, just the frame but with a wooden cover that was propped open with a stick. There was no power or water inside the home. The selling point of this particular village was the river that it bordered. The water was boiled for cooking and drinking. The river was apparently deep as it was also used to keep gallons of beverages cold, mostly palm wine, I thought, and there was a designated place downstream to bathe in and another for washing clothes. These people were very resourceful—generators were used when fuel was available and they could fix them when they broke down with little more than what they had lying around and inge-nuity. The same held true for their cars and motorcycles.

We came to a wooden picnic type table next to a big stove and fire pit, and Alusaine asked if we'd like to rest there and maybe sample a little palm wine. We told him we were carrying bottled water in the car, and that our driver would be back shortly. We sat to wait for Mohamed and I imagined what it might be like living there. A woman came up at about that time, pulled a child's red wagon loaded up with cooking utensils, and began preparing the scene for the night's cooking. A separate fire was prepared for light. The woman had the kitchen assembled in no time, and was beginning to peel something that looked like a yam. A child arrived with a second wagon in tow filled with firewood and a half-empty burlap bag of rice. Soft evening light was filtering through the horizon, and in a rare moment of respite in the up-country, I allowed my mind to wander and imagined what it might be like to live here. Could I survive as these people did?

I opened my eyes to see Alusaine coming back towards us with Mohamed following close behind. Mohamed had our duffle bags with our water and trail mix. Most of my life, water had been within arm's reach, and I was increasingly appreciative of its presence after some periods where clean water was not so readily available. Alusaine was saying he had just spoken to his father, and that he had received his father's permission to slaughter a goat for a small celebration of our arrival. It was almost too good to be true. I expected a lot of treachery and danger, especially concerning some of the posted warnings we had seen on the way in but we were receiving a warm welcome. Alusaine's intuition carried a lot of weight with the community it seemed.

Alusaine reiterated his feelings regarding our arrival. "It's fate." he said. "We will celebrate tonight and give thanks." I was a little squeamish about the goat, to be honest, and I remember seeing a couple tied to a tree as we drove in and couldn't help but wonder if the unlucky goat was one of those I had seen. Fortunately, there was no spectacle made of killing the goat. They simply led it out back by the table area, and its throat was cut and it was raised by its hind legs and dangled from a tree branch to drain the blood, which was collected in a metal pot placed under the goat's head. "I hope you like curried goat." Alusaine remarked sociably. Mohamed bounced his head up and down eagerly in a "yes" motion. Gigi and I both smiled. By the time the sun had fully set, the smell of barbecue goat was in the air and several large pots with things boiling in them sent up plumes of steam. Several gallon jugs had now been placed on the picnic table, and a tray of little wooden cups or small bowls had been placed next to them. A few people had started to gather, and a few large bamboo mats were unrolled close to the fire. People began to take seats on the mats. And as some people would come up to take a cup of palm wine, we would exchange smiles and hellos. We were able to walk over to the river and wash up with soap we had brought from the hotel. Making sure that we kept the stream water off of our lips, I used a wet bandanna to wash my face, retied my hair back into a ponytail and fished a fresh T-shirt out of the duffle bag. Gigi did more or less the same thing. I asked him what we planned to do about eating. Obviously, this was a gesture of kindness, and we didn't have to be told that not partaking could have bad consequences, but we could be risking illness if we ate. Even a bad case of diarrhea would be a very problematic thing here, we were a day away from anything.

Back at the table, Mohamed was sampling the palm wine. I could tell by the grimace on his face as he drank a cup that it was an acquired taste. I noticed he had only one though. And spent most of the night looking quietly at the fire.

The goat, which had been on a spittle slowly being turned by the woman who had brought the cooking utensils, was now being cut at a separate cooking table into shreds of appropriate size for a stew. The smell of the curry and other spices was aromatic and reminiscent of a restaurant. Alusaine began to bang a wooden spoon into a small metal pot, making a clanging noise for everyone's attention.

He addressed the small congregation of fifteen or twenty people in his tribal language but when he got to our names it was easy to figure out he was introducing us.

After he finished speaking, they responded with a smattering of applause and they began to line up for plates. A plate was placed in front of me and one in front of Gigi. I raised an empty wooden cup towards Alusaine and then towards the crowd and pretended to take a drink. Then I sat back down and without much hesitation as was custom there, I reached into my bowl with my fingers and scooped up a bite, which I then shoveled into my mouth with the aid of my thumb, I had seen this done at the hotel and at the beach bar, so I was not surprised there was no silverware. Everyone began to eat at that time, and in the same manner, I heard Gigi whisper, "You are smooth like pie." I almost choked on barely stifled laughter and a piece of goat bone. I had no idea how bony a goat could be. We made it through dinner, making it look good the whole time. Neither of us drank the wine, and we made it look at least as if we had eaten.

The fire was dwindling down and folks had state started to wander around the village. A few of those trash can fires were lit, and Alusaine settled down to speak with us.

Alusaine was very excited. He said throughout the night that he had been seeking the advice of village elders and asking those he saw interacting with us their opinion of us. He seemed very happy to report that they had all been very positive. He had a proposition for us. I knew he was an industrious, go-getter type. This guy would do well in the States, you could see his wheels were always turning. He had already put out the word and tomorrow when the sun rose, he had asked those he knew to come to his house and meet with us as buyers and sellers. Gigi and I had been very fortunate indeed.

The difference in the sort of luck we were having I think was the result of just knowing after the first trip that you had to present as humble, genuine, kind and generous. Gigi and I are both naturally empathetic people, and I had noticed that many times, Gigi and I found ourselves discussing the plight of these people and the conditions under which they had become accustomed to surviving in. And that our minds had, at times, been not on the diamonds but on the people. Somehow that made a positive difference, and this reception had been something bigger and rarer than we had at first thought. Not everyone was received this way.

Just the fact that we were in the village was a big deal, given the sign at the entrance. You don't have to announce your intentions—the villagers know instantly why you are there. If anyone reading this is going to attempt to duplicate what we did, my biggest piece of advice would be to be extra kind and humble to everyone you meet, and to be extremely patient.

Friendly as our hosts had been thus far, this was still the jungle, and alliances, portents, and friendships were subject to change without notice. Gigi and I were never out of each other's sight, we had taken some psychological approaches towards security, even though we hadn't actually done this, we had told the captain that we had registered with the American Embassy, and given them our expected destination and our date of return. We were sure that during the long discussion that occurred prior to us being admitted to the village, that fact had been included. Also I dropped it once in conversation when Alusaine had inquired as to the length of our stay.

There was no place for us to sleep, so we simply slept in the car. Mohamed slept under a tree nearby, and in the morning seemed no worse for the wear. We washed our faces and brushed our teeth with bottled water. As for our bathroom needs, we, of course, just went outside. But we did carry toilet paper and a small shovel—in case of number two, we tried to maintain a sense of decorum and we would bury it. I wasn't even missing the coffee I usually had along with a cigarette. And once again, I did not take the quinine pill. Today was going to be the reason we had come all this way.

Alusaine situated us in a thatched hut with a smooth dirt floor outfitted with a wooden table and a single chair. Bright light filtered in through the cracks in the thatch and jungle sounds provided a sound track as a small crowd coalesced on the other side of the hut's door. He had instructed those with parcels to line up outside. Gigi and he would stand watch at the door and keep me apprised of what was occurring outside.

One by one they began to arrive, the most unassuming people you could possibly imagine. Some wore no shirt, some no shoes, and then again, one walked in wearing Levi's and Nike—it was a place of contrasts. And by and large, these were happy, friendly people, who seemed to laugh easily with each other. The buying had begun, and it was fantastic, I had a loupe, a scale, and a tester with me.

I was seeing a lot of bolex stones, and I bought them all at $50 dollars a carat. I would weigh them and examine them right in front of the person who actually mined it. Not much haggling was necessary. I seemed to have hit on the going rate for rough in this region, that or I was paying much more than they expected—either way, it was working for my price point.

One by one they kept coming all day. Once in a while, Gigi would peek in through a cracked door and tell me we have a line of five or six people. I also saw a lot of industrial quality rough, which I was happy to buy at one US dollar per carat. These were easy to sell in the Seybold building as all of the cutters and jewelers used them to make diamond cutting wheels—it takes something as hard as a diamond to cut diamond. 10 or 12 dollars a carat would be easy to get, and the dollar a carat being spent here was being much appreciated. To be clear, industrial quality stones are ugly, and have a lot of inclusions. At the time yellow was not a well-liked color on diamonds. They were considered substandard. But now they are a thing. Who knows how much money we left on the table selling yellow and black stones for industrial use. If anything, it illustrates that the way wealth is stored in diamonds is somewhat capricious.

The day seemed to go by fast, and by late noon, I had spent $47k, where the bills used to be was now a respectable parcel, but I had just a couple of thousand left in cash, and it was very possible we might need to bribe our way out of one dilemma or another, so I decided that that was all we could do for this trip, and I packed up the loupe, scale and tester, and double-checked the money belt which now carried the day's diamond purchases as well as most of the remaining cash, and stepped through the door and out of the one-room shack.

The sun was hovering low. It appeared to be a flaming disk balanced delicately on the distant ridge line.

Gigi inquired, "So how did we do?"

"Very well, I think. We'll have to wait and see what we are offered back in Miami but we spent just about all the money that we brought up."

Just about that time, one more guy came up with diamonds he wished to sell. But Alusaine told him we were finished for the day. I interrupted him, and said "If it's okay with you, I don't mind taking a look."

The man hurried forward and looked like he had been traveling. Perhaps he had come from far away. Whatever he was bringing, he cupped tightly in his closed hands.

"Okay then" said Alusaine. "Show him what you have."

The man was squat, almost stubby; a coating of dust clung to his shins. Had he run here? He was clothed in the area's standard T-shirt and shorts. He looked up at me, and unfolded his hands raising them up to about my eye level.

His hands were brimming with triangular rocks, each about the size of a thumbnail. I didn't recognize them from my studies at all. They were flat, one-dimensional oddities to me. They looked more like cut glass than rough stones. I placed my bag on the ground and dug out the diamond tester. Sure enough though, they tested diamond, but what use could these possibly be. They were just flat triangles, almost like guitar picks.

"How much do you want?" I asked him.

"To me, I think I should have 25 dollars per stone, no matter the big or the small."

They did not vary that much in size but there were differences. But still this was not a stone that Ygal had taught me about. I had anxious visions of arriving with hundreds of these and hearing Ygal ask me, "Whaddya' want me to do with these?"

I was running low on money but I said to him "Give me ten of the biggest and ten of the smallest. And I peeled 5 $100 bills from the fold in my pocket. I simply put those stones into my jeans pocket, I didn't want to show the money belt out in the open. The gentleman poured the stones that remained, which was most of them back into a small purse made of some sort of fur and tied it closed with a piece of twine that he now tied to a belt loop on his cargo style shorts. The bills he placed into his hip pocket, and he gave the pocket a couple of pats on the outside with his open hand.

He seemed very pleased with himself. He told us he had been saving those for about half his life and that they were not highly regarded stones by many. But he said, if they are good for you, you will be back very soon. I smiled and agreed wholeheartedly with him, and Gigi and I both took it to mean that perhaps other would-be buyers had passed on these stones as well, which made it easier to walk away from a small mountain of them. I thought worst case scenario, they are top grade industrial, and I might make a few bucks.

Alusaine had demonstrated that there were diamonds in the area of his village, a point he no doubt had wanted to make. He was inventive and clever because he waited until after we had finished all the day's business before finally getting to the proposition he had excitedly mentioned last night.

Alusaine began to explain to us the way it works in the up-country. Normally you have to rent a tract, he explained. The village elders of the surrounding villages divide the land into tracts or parcels that they each have control over. Those tracts can be leased from the village, each village or the person who speaks for a village can set their terms and everything is negotiable but typically what they expect is for you to lease the land, make the village certain payments, not always necessarily money—it could be goods and fuel or whatever supplies were in short supply at that particular time. In return, they would mine the area you have leased. But all of that only gave you the right to buy them from the finder. So essentially, you were expected to pay for everything just for the privilege of buying what was found on your tract.

But still I was interested, very interested. Today had been a dream come true and what Alusaine was offering felt like a way to keep it going. I was already certain that we had at least tripled our money today after expenses are deducted, and there was a possibility that it could be even more. As long as the price was this low, it could be well worth it.

There were many things to discuss so we decided to stay another night in the car so that we could continue in the morning. Alusaine wanted us to have dinner with him again, and we were in no position to deny him. As is the custom, a few people were using their hands to reach into a large pot of rice. I noticed that they tended to partition small portions of the large pot, in other words the person sitting at the 9 o'clock position was not reaching into the 3 o'clock position of the pot. That made sense and we could see that it was a respected rule, but not something that we were used to doing. Fortunately there was fruit available and we ate mostly that.

Everything had been a communal effort of sorts. It seemed as if everyone pitched in to get fires and dinner going, and as soon as dinner was done, everything was whisked away. Alusaine, Gigi and I sat at the picnic table while the fire dwindled down.

We began to discuss what was required, and where it could be attained. A man it seems had rented a nearby tract, and had set some equipment there. He had managed to get a few shipping containers all the way up from the port in Freetown. He also had a fuel tanker there, which was now empty, and also a large crane. The man, it seems, had run out of money a few months back and had gone back to Europe to try to raise more. Exemplifying to us how it was always a gamble. Even if we could accomplish those same things, there was always the chance that it wouldn't pan out. It was very hard to imagine a large crane being trailered all the way up the harrowingly narrow roads cut into the side of this mountain. That must have been one hell of a feat but by the same token, it also exemplified that someone had a lot of belief in what they were doing. It could not have been easy nor could it have been cheap.

Alusaine was sure that if the man did not return, he would be able to appropriate the digging machine and his fuel tanker and all we would need then was the fuel. Perhaps smaller tankers could be dispatched from Freetown to fill it incrementally. Perhaps others would use it too, if they could provide their own fuel. Since it didn't belong to a village or a person living there, they viewed it as something that could be shared. Gigi had let me do most of the talking. We sat there discussing the possibilities till the early hours of the morning. Alusaine assured me that if we could come to a similar agreement as the ones others had attempted, ours would succeed. I was particularly struck by one thing he said during that conversation, He said, "Mr. Mark I swear to you, we will dig. If we were to find a diamond in a man's front yard today, by tomorrow morning, his house would no longer be there because we would dig it all up straight away." At that moment, for some reason I believed him.

We slept a few hours in the car and awoke with the rising sun. But we were beginning to run low on bottled water, so we washed up in the river. The water was ice cold, but it felt good to put on a fresh change of clothes. Once again I took no pill. We spent that whole day planning for what we would need in order to get started right away, and eventually reached an agreement about what we would provision Alusaine's village with in return for the rights to buy the diamonds they found. We would travel down to Freetown with Alusaine accompanying us. Mohamed knew of a money exchanger who would give us a better rate than the banks. The large purchases would have to be made in leones. We had agreed on shovels and picks and screen sifters, also, we would provide burlap bags of rice and some industrial-sized cans of cooking oil. The list was considerable and we were talking thousands of dollars to be left behind as an investment. It was agreed that Mohamed would continue to be part of the operation and a designated driver for getting things to and from Freetown. It was late in the day and we would not make it to town in time today but we could be there first thing in the morning when they opened. We knew we would be driving partly in the dark but we weren't really relishing the idea of another night in the car, so we decided to go anyway. Halfway down and well after dark, the car got a flat. And as fate would have it, there was no spare.

"How in the hell did we come up-country without a spare!" I wondered.

"I thought it was stored on the undercarriage," Gigi said.

Mohamed chimed in that someone would come either up or down the road, and we'll get help. We commenced jacking up the car in order to take the flat off and have it repaired. There was a village just a kilometer or two more down the mountain, and someone there would help him repair it. I had not yet realized that in Africa, the sky appears to have twice as many stars, and I realized it was because of the lack of light pollution. Halfway down this mountain, sitting now on the middle of a dirt and gravel road, I really saw the night sky for the first time in my life. I could actually see the curvature of the earth. It was a most amazing moment and a sight I'll never forget. Another one of those contrasts, sitting on what felt like the most desolate place on earth, I was looking at one of the most beautiful sights I'd ever seen. So bright, so clear that a few constellations actually made sense. When you are stargazing from your backyard, the constellations never look anything like the book illustrations. I was looking from the wrong perspective. For once I could see what our ancestors had been looking at, and instead of haphazardly speckled dots of light, I perceived the truly star-studded cast of characters our ancestors had been captivated by for millennia.

A jitney bus did eventually come clattering up the mountain road; they were on their way up but the driver said the bus would be coming back down in the morning. It was about 11 pm now. That wasn't great but it wasn't horrible. While Gigi snoozed in the car, Alusaine and I sat there on that mountain road passing the night discussing our business. In a way, I found myself thankful for the mishap because it gave us time for pause and we were able to discuss every detail of the business we could think of that we hadn't already covered. I made sure to hammer my key points repeatedly. I felt sure beyond a shadow of a doubt that Alusaine and I had a complete understanding. As the hours wore on, I watched as Orion plunged out of perspective followed inevitably by Canis Major, and animatedly plotted with my newfound partner in diamond mining all the while. Alusaine and I eventually passed into a light sleep just as the gods draped the grey curtain of dawn across the sky. Shortly after sunrise, I heard the rickety jitney making its way back down the mountain. Mohamed was on it with our fixed tire. Again I ignored the quinine pill.

We mounted the tire back on the car without any drama and we were back under way. We went straight to the hotel upon returning to Freetown.

Mohamed wanted to go home to check on his family, and we wanted to shower and find something to eat.

The hotel did have a good laundry service, and all the clothes from the 4 days of traveling were picked up by one of the maids and taken to be washed and pressed. We had another layer of almost Martian red dust built up on us, and Gigi and I wanted a shower. We took for granted the carpeting, the beds with their crisp sheets and comforters, the towels, the running water, even the toilets. But none of it was lost on Alusaine. He was born and raised in Sierra Leone yet he had never been in either of the two hotels in Freetown, or in any town, for that matter. After a quick shower, it felt great to be back in the hotel. I headed down to the front desk, and requested access to our safe deposit box and an envelope. Alone now in the room behind the front desk that was used for privacy, I opened the box, put the diamonds into the envelope, and sealed it. I then took the remaining $50k and placed it in the belt. Only 3 stacks of ten thousand each fit into the belt, and once again, I put ten grand in each boot. We all came down to the restaurant where we ordered cold cokes and flat bread with fried eggs and hummus. That was the last good meal I would have for over a week.

Mohamed had returned within two hours, and there was still plenty of daylight left. There was a hardware store in town that would have most of what we were looking for but first, we had to exchange dollars on the black market. Mohamed directed us to park on a busy street and wait. He would have to go alone as these were not the warm welcoming type he had to deal with. I gave him the two bricks I carried in each boot to exchange. Mohamed was gone maybe for half an hour, before I saw him coming down the street with a medium-sized box on his shoulder, he was taller than most and I could see him from a block away. When he arrived at the car, I saw that the box was filled with stacks of leones tied together with rubber bands.

"That's twenty grand? Looks like a million," I said.

"Yes." he said. "And it's only the first ten. I have to return for the other box that is being filled now."

We took our boxes of money to the hardware store. In Sierra Leone, what I'm referring to as a hardware store is more akin to an open air market, where you can find barbed wire, lumber, and tools right across from cages of live chickens or pens of livestock. You can sometimes pay for the aforementioned tools *with* chickens if you've got nothing else to work with. Anything that can rot or ruin in the rain is shielded by tarps tied to tall poles in a tent-like square and vendors sometimes take cover in the shade as well.

The money didn't last long once there—we spent it all on shovels and tools and everything we had painstakingly measured out the previous night. Also we got two brand new 7k watt Chinese generators—very highly valued in the up-country. From there, we went to the port where grain and rice were available for sale. Some of the things we purchased would be left where they were until they could be picked up, but we worked all day, we filled the Mercedes with as much as it could carry, and we made an uneventful trip up-country and delivered the first load of supplies to Alusaine's village. It was like Christmas—there was much excitement, and we genuinely felt like we were doing something good for them while trying to do something good for us as well.

We felt like we had accomplished a lot. Upon returning to the Mammy Yoko, we paid Mohamed for a job well done. Alusaine would stay the night with us, and in the morning, we would return to the hardware market to collect the remainder of our supplies and haul the last of it to the up-country. We would have them all set up to continue mining. I was reminded of those who had said to me back in the States that if it were that easy, everyone would be doing it. It was anything but easy but it was proving to be possible so far. We asked Mohamed to bring Nelson tomorrow; we could use the help. He agreed and we parted for the evening.

The hotel had added a new feature since my last visit. They had set up closed circuit TV, and you could call the front desk and request a title. If they had the movie available, it would be played on a VCR downstairs and piped to your room. We settled down in the room and we ordered *Rambo* for Alusaine, at his request. I had never seen someone so enthralled by the things we take for granted. Alusaine was clearly having the time of his life, and it was infectious—Gigi and I started having the time of our life as well.

CHAPTER 6

The next morning, he was still talking about the movie and how much fun the hotel had been. I wished I could bring him to the States—even just a digital gas pump with its blue number display would seem dazzling to him. I'm sure, eventually, it would become old hat to him too, but it would be great fun watching it happen. Mohamed pulled up alone, Gigi asked Mohamed "Where's Nelson?"

That's when we all noticed the look on his face. Nelson had been killed last night—stabbed in the heart, over some matter involving $80 US.

We had a mostly silent ride back up the mountain. Gigi and I were quiet out of respect for Mohamed, who was having a hard time with it at the moment. The two had been friends since grade school. It had begun to rain, which seemed fitting at the time.

We were negotiating the checkpoints with ease. We were still getting the shake down but it was insignificant amounts. 5 or 10 leones were doing the trick, that and Alusaine speaking up for us, almost like he was taking responsibility for us. We had spent most of that twenty grand, and counting the money had been a bit of a hassle. The two generators had cost about 9000 USD, and that had been almost an entire box of leones. But the government was very serious about using only the local currency. They wanted your money to be good only at the exchange houses or the banks. And when you left, they didn't like you taking the currency out with you, which wasn't usually a problem as no one was investing in leones.

The rain was continuing to fall, and suddenly, there were torrents of water headed downhill. Mohamed began to look a little concerned, as the car would sometimes begin to spin tires and do a bit of sideways sliding—it would be very easy to go sliding right off the road and into the bush. Gigi wanted to take over the driving, and I agreed. I was sitting in the front with Mohamed, and I asked him to stop the car and apply the parking brake as soon as we got to a little patch of road where the tires had grip. The car had made it this far up the mountain because it was loaded down with supplies and the extra weight and the four of us inside helped to give it traction. There were two generators on a skid tied to the roof, the trunk contained about 500 pounds of rice and there were odds and ends back there as well.

I told Mohamed that Gigi was here with me because he had certain talents, one of them was just watching my back, and another was his driving skills. Gigi could and had driven most things with wheels—he could drive a big rig, a backhoe, a forklift. He was a hell of a snow driver too, and right now I needed him behind the wheel.

"You've got a lot on your mind, which is to be expected. Let us worry about getting up the rest of the way," I said. Mohamed agreed with what I perceived to be a little bit of relief actually.

The rain had really intensified, and Alusaine thought we should just stay in that spot we were stopped at until the rain stopped. But there was no telling how long that could be, and Gigi made the case that the road could just begin to wash away—or worse, the mountain above us could wash away and take us with it. Gigi started the car and put it in gear. It seemed like we went a few feet, and then suddenly it felt like we were on skates again. Gigi was accelerating a lot more aggressively than Mohamed had been, and was struggling to keep the car pointed up hill. At times, we could hear the tires spinning on the clay as it flung up grey, wet sand in all directions but the car was either not moving or worse it would begin to slide towards the edge of the road. We were guaranteed three to four violent rolls down the mountain if that happened. It was now too dark and there was too much rain to see what was down there but I knew we didn't want to find out. The motor was really getting a work out and to get some traction, Gigi kept moving to the shoulder. I was not a fan of the idea and kept yelling at him to be careful and that he was too close. A few times he looked worried himself. Suddenly behind where we had just passed, a portion of the road just washed away almost like if you were hosing dirt down your driveway—it just simply began to all slide downhill. The water was now gaining momentum washing down the middle of the road as well, and little raging waterfalls were forming here and there. I asked Gigi if we should abandon the car, to which he responded we may not have a choice. Bushes, vegetation, debris and branches were washing down the road. The tires on that Mercedes were not only not good, they weren't even matched, but somehow we started getting a little traction. Luckily it seemed that branches and exposed rocks were giving the tires something to grip. Slowly we continued advancing and ascending. We were just pulling into the village when the old Mercedes decided it had had enough, and completely seized up. With a huge puff of smoke like a cough, the car sputtered then rattled, and then just hissed. The four of us looked at each other. Gigi turned to look at Mohamed and Alusaine, and ever the good sport, he cheerfully remarked, "You guys won't be allowed back in the village. Look at you—you have both turned white."

I am not sure why but it seemed a lot funnier than maybe it should have, and we all laughed for a few minutes like it was the funniest thing ever. The rain was still coming down hard, but it felt a lot less threatening being stopped and out of the car. We realized though that we didn't know any other way down.

We walked the rest of the way into the village. Alusaine did not want to take any chances. He began to rouse a few men who had been sleeping. Among the things we had purchased, we had gotten batteries and flashlights as well as gas lanterns. Those things were put to use immediately. I had brought one of the flashlights with me and Gigi had one as well. Alusaine had found us a place to stay with a couple he said were part of his family although he didn't say how. We could use their living room. There would be no bed but there was netting to keep the bugs off you, which he assured us, would be trying to make their way to dryer spots during the rest of this night. Out of our duffle bags which we had carried from the car, we were able to change into dry clothes, and we actually slept on that dirt floor with our bags and pillows. Mohamed was taken to the one-room shack where we had bought the diamonds. Alusaine brought him a change of clothes and evidently took care of him. I thought it was a good thing if they were bonding and getting along, as I planned for Mohamed to be the driver and to work closely with Alusaine when we were gone.

By the time we made it back to the car the next morning, all of the supplies had been brought into the village. One of the things we had purchased was water pumps for moving the water out of the holes they had dug in order to wash the gravel.

I could now see two of them being moved from across the village. I knew they were ours 'cause you could see the new hoses with the price ticket still hanging from it and the pumps looked brand new. And just like that they were mining, for themselves yes, but also for us. Mohamed tried starting the Mercedes but I'm not sure why. It had clearly fought its final valiant fight last night and died as it reached the gates.

I knew what was troubling Mohamed, and it was then that I told him, "I've been planning to buy you a proper car to drive for our new company anyway. What was the cost of the old Mercedes?"

Visibly relieved that I was broaching the issue, he replied, "My brother-in-law paid $800 US dollars one year ago for this thing."

"Well, he drove it for a year, and I'm guessing you did too. Here's $500 for your brother-in–law, and we avoid any tears."

Mohamed grinned, "That works for me."

But now we had to figure out a way back down to Freetown. A man came walking up the road and we asked him how conditions were down below. He said it was only passable by foot; the sudden and heavy rain had caused a narrow part of the river to crest, and it had created a flash flood. A village below had lost some homes but reportedly no one was hurt.

"The men from that village that are down at the point where the road washed away say that you have brought shovels and picks. We would like to use some of them to fix the road so that cars may once again pass."

"I would love to say yes myself but you will have to ask Alusaine. He is in charge of all of that now. He's just up the way in front of his house."

The man bid us farewell and was off.

Of course, I realized now that we were stranded, even if we had a car, the road would be impassable. We headed back to the village not really knowing our next move.

And it looked like rain was going to be a problem once again today.

We sat on the dirt floor of the hut Mohamed had slept in the night before. We were sharing our last pack of cigarettes. We were out of trail mix, and we had two bottles of water left. We were slowly coming to the realization that the only way we could get down would be by walking. But that was not as easy as it sounded, and we had to bear in mind that we were a long way from anything. So the slightest injury could quickly compound into something more serious. At least our duffles were not that heavy as they now contained no water.

In the up-country, when something like this happens, all of the villages come together for the common good, and as a result, sometimes they can accomplish the seemingly impossible. We decided to wait and see what tomorrow would be like, and hoped that maybe the men would repair the road.

The rainy season was indeed upon us and I hate to admit it but I hadn't thought or considered that there even was a rainy season. But in Africa, I definitely should have. The continuing rain made it difficult for the men who were laboriously trying to clear the debris with manual labor. And with the shovels Alusaine had provided, they were trying to build up the road once again. No mining was taking place and that was making me edgy.

Two long mostly rainy days followed. We ate the plain white rice gratefully but were running short on water. On the third day, we decided we had no choice but to attempt the walk. It was Tuesday already of the second week, and our flight that we had hoped to be on was in two days. We still owed Mohamed a car. I decided and they agreed that the three of us would walk down.

The going was slow under an oppressively hot tropical sun. It felt as though the sun's rays were being magnified by a celestial microscope and the lingering humidity coupled with swarming insects only increased the seeming assault of the elements. But in about two hours, we had made it past the washout, and were now standing on a gravel road once again. We remarked that the going would be easier from here but we were wrong. About another quarter mile down the mountain road, the gravel disappeared under a small mountain of mud. This was a much scarier event than we had thought. Gigi had definitely made the right decision. We were now pretty sure that this was the spot where both Mohamed and Alusaine had wanted to put rocks under the back tires and wait it out with the car in park. We would have no doubt washed down into the gulch with everything else. Gigi had made an excellent choice, and I was lucky.

We had been walking for hours but still we estimated from what we could see below us that we were not even half way down yet. It was getting dark but we finally made it back to the gravel road. We had no choice but to continue walking but I was grateful for the road. I was beginning to feel nauseous again, and I thought it was from not eating again for most of the day. As we rounded a switchback, the flickering fire lights of a village came into view. There was a narrower road that diverged off the main road, and we followed it right to a village center—a square, if you will. There seemed to be nothing but men in the square, which seemed poorly lit. There was a statue or an empty fountain of some sort right in the middle of the square but people were hanging out on it. I couldn't tell what it had ever been, but it looked like it used to be a place of some importance—a village square, a church yard or something, I just couldn't tell. The men were mostly young, and the few trash can fires were burning kind of low and not providing much light perhaps due to the lack of dry wood to burn. All I knew was that I was hungry and needed to find something to eat. There was a cantina-style shack on one side of the square, and a few men were hanging out under its open awning. I walked over to take a look, and right away, I noticed two things of interest: there were dusty cans of sardines—the type you open with a key that comes attached to the can. I immediately asked and paid for two of the red flat cans, using the key and without stepping away from the counter I peeled back the first lid and I began to voraciously eat the sardines with my fingers. I finished the first can in some sort of record time, and grabbed the second can and made short work of it too. It wasn't until I had finished the second can that I noticed that all the men in the square including Gigi were staring at me. I remember looking up and seeing all of these faintly illuminated tribes people with their eyes fixed on me. I must have appeared like a spirit that had wandered out of the jungle—that or a famished animal from the same place. I didn't exactly know what to do at that moment, so I just asked the guy behind the counter if there was a trash receptacle to which he replied, "I'll take care of it."

As I walked away I could still feel the eyes upon me. Gigi said, "You looked like a ravenous beast, standing there in the middle of everyone with your duffle bag still hanging on you, eating fish scales and all. I'm surprised you didn't lick the empty tin can but it seemed like you might take a bite of it too."

"I felt a lot of respect for you," he said. "You looked like a man who does what he has to do."

"Thanks, it's just that I've been feeling a little nauseous, and thought I was getting a little dizzy. I felt like I had to eat fast," I said.

"So how do you feel now?"

"Much better." I said. "Let's see what we can do to get out of here."

Mohamed came through the crowd with a man in tow. As he approached, he said, "Mr. Mark, Mr. Gigi, this man has offered to take you into Freetown for fifty dollars US."

I couldn't see the stars, so I knew it had to be cloudy and that rain was probable. We still had quite a ways to go, so I agreed. We gave the man a fifty-dollar bill, and put our duffles in his trunk. It was some economy size

POS; I never got a look at it in the daylight. I hoped our luck was changing. We pulled out of the square and onto the main road heading down. I
don't know if the driver was drunk, crazy, suicidal—perhaps all three. All I
know is that from the moment we hit the road, he was pushing the little car
as fast as it would go. It felt like we were on one of those traveling carnival
roller-coasters that set up in a parking lot in small towns that you don't quite
trust, the kind that makes you sign a waiver before riding. Maybe he was just
trying to show his superior driving skills and his knowledge of the mountain,
but the little car was screaming and careening down the sloped road like a
streak of liquid mercury. Gigi was in the front seat with the speed demon,
and Mohamed and I were in the back seat. Each of us was holding on to the
little head rest on the seat in front of us and I remember Mohamed and I
glanced at each other and both of us had looks of grave concern and worry.
I was about to scream, or maybe yell at the driver to slow down, but just as
I opened my mouth to say something, a loud gunshot scared the shit out of
me. Only it wasn't a gunshot, it was the front driver side tire exploding. The
four of us practically instinctively dived to the right of the car as if we were
avoiding a grenade. Our collective recoil was a movement so sudden and
forceful that it may have kept the little bucket of bolts from running off the
road and tumbling down the side of the mountain. As it was, the car came
to a sideways stop at the top of the embankment and it appeared to have dug
into the soft mud just off the right side of the road. From the passenger side
windows, you could see over the precipice into the gloomy darkness below.
Mohamed was the first out of the car. He screamed at the driver, "Man you
craze, you gon' kill every one! Where you learn to drive? Give me back the
man's money."

He looked as if he was getting set to hit him. The man had not said a
word yet, but he fumbled for his wallet and handed the fifty back to Mohamed.
We asked him to open the trunk so we could get our bags out. The ride had
lasted under half an hour, nonetheless we'd descended too far to go back up
and find someone else to drive us, but we were still far from Freetown. We left
the man and his broken down car, and began the trudge down the mountain,

our path illuminated by flashlights. We walked until sunup and again it was a jitney headed down that saved us.

I was getting pretty feverish and barely made it into the room back at the Mammy Yoko before I threw up in the toilet. I came out of the bathroom and washed up, thinking I felt a bit better. "Gigi, I need to lie down for a minute. Here's the key to the safety deposit box. Both our names are on the register. Just make sure everything's alright please."

Gigi sized me up while I flopped down on the mattress. "You better lie down alright. You are looking pale," he said.

That's about when the second wave of nausea hit me. I closed my eyes hoping that would help, and said, "Gigi, I think I got food poisoning from the sardines last night." He agreed that I must have. I was back in the bathroom throwing up a second time when everything just went blurry, and the next thing I knew I was on the bathroom floor.

"Hey, hey! Can you hear me? What happened?" it was Gigi standing over me. He helped me to sit up just in time to give me a chance to lurch at the toilet bowl, but I didn't quite make it. After the third time throwing up, it just became a blur. It wasn't long until I had severe diarrhea as well as vomiting and I was burning up. I guess I had begun to make a mess, but it was still early morning, and the maids were out in the hallways doing their rooms. Gigi requested extra towels to clean up my mess but the maid insisted she would clean. "Just lie down in the bed for ten minutes and I'll have it ready for you," she said. If I were well, my pride would never have allowed anyone to look after me that way but as it was, I gave her the fifty Mohamed had snatched back from the speed demon, as I went towards the bed.

"Thank you very much."

That was the last thing I remember her saying. I told Gigi, "I'll be okay by tomorrow. Take care of the situation with Mohamed. Just leave me in the bathroom, I'll be fine." But I wasn't fine. In fact, I was getting worse. I spent a hellish night alternating between projectile vomiting and squirting out of my ass the way a horse pees, too weak to keep going between the bed and the toilet I was just lying on the bathroom floor between bouts. Midway through that next morning, I remember hearing Gigi telling me we are going to have to miss our flight. I guess it was mid-morning when I heard the maid back in the room talking to Gigi. The bathroom was a mess again, and there was no getting me out to clean it.

"That man does not have food poisoning," I heard the maid say. "That poor man has a case of malaria. He needs to go to the hospital."

The next thing I remember is, it was dark again. Gigi was moving me around trying to clean and he had gotten pedialyte and salt tablets. He put tablets in the pedialyte and literally tried to pour it into me.

I started hallucinating at some point. I have no explanation why, but I relived my 7th grade year in total. I hallucinated everything in vivid detail, and memories I didn't even know I had, emerged. I was on the bathroom floor for the better part of four days, and I remember Gigi saying he was going to use the medical evacuation insurance. I remember just resisting and saying no, we have to finish what we started. He kept saying, "If you're not better tomorrow, I'm going to do it, I don't care what you say." "Don't you dare, don't dare," I remember saying to him. He kept pouring the pedialyte down me. It was a whole week before I was able to get up one day. Standing leaning on a dresser with a mirror on it, I could see the definition of my bones, my ribs were protruding, my face was gaunt and pale, my eyes were sunken, with black circles underneath them. Holy shit, I thought, how close did I come to dying?

"I guess we missed our flight," I said with a laugh that made my stomach hurt—my muscles were sore from the convulsing.

"Twice," Gigi responded dryly.

"I'm sorry"

"It's okay—I took care of everything while you were having fun. But seriously, I took care of the car with Mohamed, I called everyone that needed calling, including my job, I spoke to Eli. He wanted me to evac you out too, but I told him how you were being, and he said you better leave him then."

We laughed again and it hurt again. Something about Africa was bringing out the best in me, and I realized I was very grateful to be alive. Maybe it was just the cloud nine of a narrow brush with an undignified death.

We had another whole week, and I had been out a whole week. It felt a little surreal to be up and around again, I felt as if I had just come out of a fantasy world. I had a strange appreciation for everything—the sunlight, the ocean, my friend who had spent an entire week administering pedialyte and salt tablets. I felt strangely lucky and even colors seemed brighter. It was good coming out of that fog.

CHAPTER 7

T he road had been repaired to a degree, and it was at least passable. I was amazed at what could be done with shovels and manpower; no machinery or gas-powered tools had been used. Mohamed and Gigi had found an old Nissan Pathfinder, for US$4k. It appeared to be in great shape and had customized undercarriage protection. This was a proper work vehicle and nicer than anything I had at home. We had found the vehicle just in time as the old car would not be able to handle the road in its present condition.

It seemed a lot of things in Sierra Leone were dilapidating quickly. There was a non-operational television station, the gas station pumps had all since broken and a hand pump had to be used to dispense gasoline, there was no federal entity to fix the roads… There was a lot I should have seen coming, but from my perspective at the time, these hardships appeared to just be part of normal life. But that wasn't the case with the people who had been living there for the last 18 years, as they were experiencing the collapse of infrastructure and economic decline in real time and a real resentment was building.

The trip took an additional two hours, and more than once, it seemed that the Nissan would get stuck. The going had become really rough and rain in the afternoons now appeared to be an everyday phenomenon. The road had continued to wash away as the villagers continued to struggle to keep clearing it as well as building it back up. The work was hard and it was dirty but they did it.

We arrived at the village and it was late afternoon already. Alusaine said the work was slow as we had no fuel, even though Gigi and Mohamed had brought a hundred gallons during the week I was sick. Our new tools were mostly deployed with the road fixers as were our pumps and that's where most of the fuel had been used as well.

I was not happy, and I said so to Alusaine, "This is not part of our deal. We didn't agree to be responsible for the entire mountain!"

Alusaine countered, "If we cannot use the road, we cannot survive, we can't transport anything down or up."

I knew he was right, but I had expected to see something. I explained to him we were not an endless source of funds. I didn't mention the two and a half bricks I still had in the money belt. "We are on what you might call a very tight budget. There is no built-in room for expenses of this sort."

He didn't quite seem to get on the same page with me for the first time that day. To him, the newly developed problem of the road was a perfectly good reason to adjust our deal. Gigi and I looked at each other and we both seemed to be thinking the same thing.

"We are going to need more fuel. It's clear that bringing it 50 or 100 gallons at a time won't be cost efficient or sufficient." I asked Alusaine about the man who had hauled up the large fuel tanker. He said the man had not been seen for months. So status quo there. But he said there was a logging camp another half-day drive away, and they had fuel transporters and heavy duty trailers and all manner of machinery. Perhaps a deal of some sort could be reached with them.

The rain was starting and once again Gigi and I were sleeping in our transportation, but it was a lot more comfortable than the old car had been.

As the sun rose, the sky was a beautiful blue but our muddy surroundings told us this was false advertising on the part of Mother Nature. We wasted no time in alerting Alusaine and Mohamed of our decision to go speak with the logging company on the other side of the mountain.

"What do we do about checkpoints?"

Alusaine shook his head "You should not encounter any. They are mostly on the Freetown side. Anyway, you've become good at dealing with them.

Just do it the same way—they are always open for business." Alusaine and Mohamed both laughed.

As was to be expected, the going was rough, and the only map we had was a hand-drawn scribble from Mohamed and Alusaine, neither of whom had been sure about what they were saying. But generally, we knew we needed to continue higher up this side to a road that corkscrewed around and to the other side of the top of this mountain. Easy enough right?

I think we found the switchback road but we wound up going down the entire way. We had seen no other roads that we could take; could we have missed it? At the bottom of the back of the mountain we had come from, the landscape was totally different. It was a flat valley that had once been filled with trees, but was a landscape of high brown grass, which obscured the hundreds of tree trunks scattered about that had been cut by the partially automated machines that just drive along grabbing the trees with mechanical arms, sawing and stripping the trunks and then throwing the harvested lumber into a pile for yet another machine to pick up. It was an expansive stretch of land that ended in a border with Guinea. Far to the south of where we were was the border with Liberia, which was held captive in the oppressive grip of Prince Johnson. We were driving along slowly on no particular road or path, but Gigi thought there had to be another road going back to the mountain. It was really difficult gauging how far around the mountain we had come. It's possible we could be lost, I thought. If we kept going north or northeast or east for that matter, we would cross into Guinea.

Being very careful with the stumps, we praised the wisdom of the previous owner of the Nissan for outfitting it with undercarriage armor and a tail pipe extension that brought the exhaust up high off the back of the body. As long as it wasn't submerged, you might make it through water that would otherwise drown your car. Fortunately we weren't testing that theory, at the moment at least.

The afternoon rains were beginning but Gigi's instinct had been right—we made it to a road that was said to lead up to a village. We only knew this because we had come upon a group of children. They were young, maybe as young as 5 or 6 to about 12 or 13. It was their village that was up that gravel road and the road continued but these children were not aware of a logging camp. When I asked how far, one child just answered, "Far, very far." I couldn't say exactly how many children the group comprised but there were both boys and girls. Many wanted to touch my hair. I was probably the first white person many of them had seen in their lives. They looked at the both of us like we were a strange species but were friendly and well-mannered. Gigi and I knew we shouldn't have done this but we asked the children to stand in a semicircle and face the camera and to hold up the middle finger of either hand and to shout "hello". We snapped the photograph of that moment, but it has since been lost unfortunately. We explained to them that it was a good way to greet all foreigners. I have no idea why we did that. I hope it wasn't too harmful, and if by the grace of the universe, one of you ever reads this, I hope you remember us and that you've had a good life.

That wasn't all we left them with. Like a good capitalist, I gave them all fives and singles to take home. We kept off-roading, I told Gigi that it was a bad sign that they had never seen white people as it meant there were no logging trucks or machines being driven here. But just as night fell, and a few hours away from the children but exactly how far I do not know, we came upon a group of men, and at about the same time the landscape changed from grass and hidden stumps to a lush, beautiful forest again. The men were not from Sierra Leone. They were refugees from Liberia. I remember one man that I got out of the truck to speak with had eyes that looked like he was in shock—wide with that mile-long stare. As we began conversing, I noticed he wasn't the only one with that look. They told us that Prince John-son was basically executing a portion of his own citizens. Gigi and I looked at each other as they spoke. They had seen some pretty atrocious things… People being mutilated and their extremities being used to decorate trees in the garden of the palace of the prince, arms and legs dangling off every branch. They shuddered at the recollection. They had fled in terror. No country had come to their aid.

"Where are the Americans?" a man amongst the group implored emotionally. "Where is the UN and their forces?"

I certainly could not give them an answer, except to respond, "I don't think America gets involved unless you have something that they want."

One gentleman piped up, "You are right, mister. On the rare occasion when we see a fighter jet, we point and laugh at the pilot who lost his way to Iraq."

I laughed along with them. It was kind of funny, I thought, but a bit of a sad commentary. These men had come across most of the country. Their journey had begun far south of where we were presently.

The rain was light but steady. Gigi and I had both been wearing baseball caps the whole trip, now the brims were a steady curtain of drips and drops. Yes, there was a logging camp but they were very far up the mountain and we had come too far around. It was completely dark but there was a near full moon and the silhouette of the mountains and the plains and the forest all in one panoramic view was one of the most beautiful sights I had ever seen. The fact that we could see the stars made us believe the rains would be ending or be sporadic and light. However, the loggers were not known to be a very welcoming group of people. The entire operation was fenced in, and trespassers, blacks or whites, were not welcome.

We decided to disregard this, as we did with most things that didn't agree with our plan. As far as we were concerned, there was nothing we couldn't do. Especially here the straight-up truth I had found was that a humble atti-tude and an open wallet pretty much got you everything and anything you needed. I had been right so far. We got directions from the men, whose only warning was that the rainy season was starting and the road may or may not be there. It was the latter that came true. We made it up the mountain a considerable distance and we were actually closer than we thought but sure enough the road just ended. There was nothing but debris and little moun-tains of black dirt about a foot tall in no particular pattern.

We had to try to find where the road went or where it was supposed to be. It must pick up somewhere. This wasn't in a Hollywood movie. Being totally alone, with no communication, no real idea of where you are can inspire all the fear and anxiety of a cinematic shootout, and then some I'm sure. The tank was empty, and Gigi and I had to get out in the drizzle to fill it. We had two ten gallon tanks attached to the back doors. I continued to feel a kinship with the previous owner of the Pathfinder. The contents of the two tanks put the needle back on 'F', and somehow that inspired some confidence in us. We began to just crawl up the mountain, stopping frequently to stand on the truck's front bumper and look for anything to orient us, whether it be a light or a road. We would start to creep up again each time at an angle left and right advancing in a zig-zag then the truck would lose traction, and it would slide down a bit. One step forward, two steps back…that sort of thing. It doesn't sound harrowing but it truly was. After having gone by a conservative estimation a quarter mile, the Nissan fell perfectly into a ditch between two large clods of dirt that just couldn't be avoided, and it was stuck, good and proper. We had burnt almost a quarter tank of gas trying to clutch it out. We had no choice but to walk, and still we didn't know where we were going.

For the first time ever I think, Gigi and I began to blame each other for this colossal fucking blunder. So we were walking and blaming each other—and this part should be in a movie—there was light from a farmhouse inside what looked to be a large compound. We had found the logging camp—we had come to within 1/8 of a mile from the front gate. Suddenly we were happy and congratulating each other again. It felt like a huge victory. We walked up to the front gate and called out a greeting through the iron bars. From the other side, an older, black man sporting a full white beard hobbled towards us hurriedly. He hunched over as he walked, as though he had borne heavy burdens most of his time. He called for someone else and a young guy came running over behind the old man. They said that "diamond people" were not allowed here. We hadn't even spoken to them yet, so I informed them that we are not looking for diamonds but fuel, and that we were stranded. That was my old philosophy coming back up, put 80% truth in every lie. I gave my left pocket a tap and added, "We have money." The old man said something to the young one. Nodding vigorously, the young man spun on his heels and melted back into the darkness towards the house.

The gatekeeper's eyes flashed back in my direction and he asked, "Where is your car?"

"Not far at all. It's in sight, actually." I said as I oriented my high-powered flashlight in the general direction of the broken down Pathfinder and the reflectors shined back at us. The old man rose his hand in a halting motion and said, "Right, okay, stop then. Don't shine the light in the bush."

Just then his younger companion materialized behind him with someone else in tow. "Let's go have a closer look at the problem." As we walked the eighth of a mile back towards the road, I could see we were only about a football field away from where the road began again. The old man scolded me a second time, asking me to not shine any light into the bush. They took a look at the car and agreed it was too stuck for the five of us alone. We headed back towards the house. One of the young men was speaking in a dialect that sounded like the Creole spoken in Haiti and often heard in Miami. Gigi picked up on it right away and began speaking to the man in French. He quickly found out that this logging camp was operated by French Nationals. The group happily conversed with Gigi, who requested that the site manager be made aware that a fellow country man was at the gate. The wrought iron gates parted with a burdensome groan and we were waved in past the threshold. "So that the lions you have called do not eat you," quipped the most senior fellow with a wry smile, and they dispersed. After just a few minutes waiting inside the gates, a middle aged Frenchman introduced himself to Gigi with what I assume was a hearty good evening. He wore Khaki overalls that appeared hastily thrown over some night-time apparel. He had a light brown beard and short, cropped, slightly receding hairline and looked like the typical construction worker. He indicated towards me with a calloused hand as Gigi spoke for both of us in French, giving our names and nationalities. I rated a very quick hello and was pretty much ignored the rest of the conversation but I was happy to see that the exchange between him and Gigi was good-mannered and spirited in spite of the late hour.

After he invited us into the camp, before I knew it, I was in a cozy room, really sparse and all wood plank but nice—I liked it. I spotted a shower and immediately appreciated its presence. I realized it was meant to be a bath as there was no shower curtain, but I wasn't feeling it so I showered and after I had dried myself, I dried the entire bathroom with my towel. Leaving it pretty much the way I found it, minus one towel.

Outside my room, I could hear Gigi and our host deep in conversation as their voices resounded in a common area. I think Gigi washed up in another room because when I emerged, he was already in new clothes and stationed at a small dining area. Dinner was being placed on the table in front of him. There was a bottle of Cognac open on the table. Gigi looked at me and sort of shrugged a 'what can I do?' type shrug. I just winked at him. It was easy to see the guy was missing friends. They talked before, during and after dinner. I couldn't understand a word, but for the hospitality I was grateful. I was being totally excluded from the conversation, so I excused myself at the next opportunity, which was the second and last time our entertainer acknowledged me with a quick nod. Gigi had an impressive school career to brag about. He had majored in finance and could speak not only of France as though he were a native but of the surrounding countries as well. They were enthralled in conversation and I'm sure the Cognacs weren't hurting. I decided to go for a walk about the place without really asking permission, I will admit I was feeling a little American at the time. There was a picnic table just outside the kitchen but outdoors nonetheless. As I walked out, I recognized one of the men who had checked on the Pathfinder with us. I inquired what they were doing eating out here.

"This is where the help eats," replied one man at the table.

They had been having dinner at the same time as us but they were eating outside. It wasn't at this precise moment but it had been raining, so I had to ask, "Are you not allowed to eat inside?"

"No." the man replied easily.

"What about when it rains?"

"We wait for it to stop," they replied with a laugh. I didn't want to get on our host's bad side. We needed him and we needed to be able to pay him to not only supply us with fuel but to deliver it to the other side of the mountain. But I was thinking about the men who had given us directions here, and what they had said about this company's usual guarded demeanor. He made it clear how he felt about Americans, and seeing the Africans forced to eat outside was reminiscent of a completely backward time in my own country. On top of that the Frenchman could just as easily have conversed in English, I'm sure. At the same time, I had to be glad that Gigi was completely willing to play along and I could trust that he hadn't forgotten our purpose. I kept strolling the perimeter. It was turning into a beautiful early morning. It was still very dark maybe 2 am or 2:30 am. The stars glittered with the mesmerizing clarity I have only seen in Africa. The ground was faintly illuminated by the yellow light from within the main hall that I could hear was powered by a single generator. There were surrounding buildings but they were dark and appeared empty. There were a few separate cabanas that orbited the house as well as a large wooden building I assumed was a mill, and as I was taking it all in, I rounded a corner, and there, sitting on a porch on a wooden stool was a guy. He was just sitting there like a ghost, and there appeared to be two boxes—large wooden boxes—flanking him one on each side, they formed a V and he was sitting in the narrowest part of the inside of the V. He didn't say a word at first. There was no electric glow here, just moonlight. It was a full moon night but that was it, and this is where it gets surreal as anything.

For me and in my memory, this is like a dream sequence. I realized the two boxes sitting on saw horses were two caskets. From this point, I can't remember the conversation verbatim. I can remember the sound of his voice but I don't know in what sequence the following information was delivered. He said the boxes contained the body of his best friend in one and the body of his brother in the other. They were friends and co-workers in some city California—no disrespect intended—I just can't remember what city he said. I know he said they were drywall hangers and surfers, they had saved twenty grand between them, and had had the same idea I had had—come to Africa and buy illicit diamonds and quadruple your money, maybe start a small-time smuggling operation with the cooperation of some villagers. But they had simply wandered into the wrong village where they were told to surrender all their money. They resisted and two of them were dead.

All I could do was sit and listen and I was in shock myself just walking up on this temporary morgue and seeing these fellow Americans was shocking. I sat there with him in silence for a while. From time to time, we could hear laughter from the house. It was surreal. Dawn was just starting to arrive when I heard the two-man party breaking up. I told the guy I'm really sorry for your loss, I hope you make it home safe. And I headed back to the house. The bottle was empty in the middle of the table. But Gigi didn't look drunk. He had a key in his hand and he said, "Follow me." I asked where our host was and Gigi said he had passed out on the couch but he was fine. "Don't talk now. Wait until we are inside," Gigi said. So I followed him. We went into one of the cottages. It looked nice and was surprisingly big—two bedrooms and a bathroom. I wondered if they were all the same and why were they empty?

Each room had a four-poster bed, and each bed had mosquito netting over it. Gigi and I decided to sleep in the same bed for security reasons. I was still carrying a lot of money. We kept our shoes with us inside the netting but we slept with our clothes on, on top of the existing bed covers. There was no electricity in the cabanas, so we had to use flashlights to go to the bathroom. It would be dark for a couple of more hours. All around that area, it seemed that there was an infestation of black scorpions and these scorpions were aggressive. For some reason, if you shined your flashlight, it attracted them, and you could hear their little claws clacking on the wood floor as they ran towards you, if of course you happened to be inside a room with wood floors, as I was presently answering the call of nature when I learned that fascinating fact. To my credit I had made sure to put my boots on before walking to the bathroom, which it seemed had no running water. Anyway I thwarted the attacker with a well-aimed stomp that produced a too loud, sickening crunch, and practically vaulted back to the safety of the mosquito net. Gigi snickered as a I crashed back into the netting "A fine *jeté*, " he said, comparing me to a ballerina apparently. "We can't talk now but I took care of it. Trust me, we will talk tomorrow," he said, and rolled over away from me. That was good enough for me, so I tried to close my eyes and get a couple of hours' sleep but I kept hearing things hitting the mosquito netting and every time I did, I would quickly train my flashlight on it and every time that I would do so, there would be some new and terrifying type of bug. Gigi was experiencing pretty much the same thing. I think we both finally fell asleep for maybe 90 minutes. And we were both relieved when the sun rose.

Last night was like a bad dream, and today the world looked full of promise. I tried not to think about the 3 Americans nonetheless I couldn't help but ask Gigi, "Did you hear about the other Americans?"

He nodded a brief affirmation and said it was better if we waited to talk. Still, I was okay with that. I splashed my face with water and looked at the large corpse of my pre-dawn attacker. This was a serious bug. Mohamed had told us about a woman who had been stung by one of these creatures, and rather than endure the pain, she had jumped off a nearby precipice to her death. Outside, one of the workers was pulling the Nissan out with a track hoe. What a wonderful appreciation a hostile jungle can evoke for a piece of landscaping equipment! It just eats the debris, flings the rocks, breaks the branches, and demolishes the moguls. All the obstacles of nature that had snared us were child's play to this machine.

As I watched them pull the Pathfinder out Gigi asked me to go get one whole brick for him. So I entered the little cottage again and took one brick out, spreading the remainder out thinner around the belt at my waist. With the amount of weight I had lost and with a shirt on, you couldn't see anything at all. I straightened up in the bathroom mirror and by the time I got back outside, the car was free. Over to the left about 300 feet, this road went higher and to another pass we could take to get home, always of course assuming it hasn't washed away. There was another flat track used for loading and moving wood that was now being loaded with the two pine boxes. Last night wasn't a dream. The surviving brother sat in the cab of the machine with his head hanging down. I couldn't see his face, just his sandy hair as it fell forward and covered his face. The Frenchman had coffee at the picnic table and he called Gig over¡. I had no expectation of being a focal point in the conversation but I decided to include myself anyway. As we approached him but without him seeing, I passed the ten grand to Gigi, which he simply placed unfolded in his back pocket so that one third of it was visible if you were standing behind him. As we walked up to the table, I stayed just behind Gigi. The conversation continued in French as I watched the half-track make its way down the road, the morbid epiphany suddenly struck me that the surviving brother had come here with the bodies specifically for the pine boxes. I wondered which village had been the village that robbed and killed them, and if we ourselves had passed through it. Nelson's death for 80 USD seemed very senseless; this was no better. During the course of casual French conversation, Gigi handed the guy the whole brick, and I wondered what the hell we had just bought for ten grand. He was at least getting a receipt signed, and it all looked and sort of sounded above board. Our host drew us a much better map of the surrounding area in greater detail. He had traveled this route as recently as yesterday and assured us it was safe and we should be able to make the other side well before nightfall if we left now. In Africa, it seemed to me everything took a day. There were very few sections of road where you could actually get going fast, and by fast I just mean 50mph.

The French logger had run that company with his family for almost twenty years. When peace had come to Sierra Leone, things had been different and business had been good. That entire area of tall grass and stumps we passed over was logged by him and his family. But with the American and Western European mining companies splitting the people against each other as well as a corrupt national government that rendered them no support, tribes had begun warring for control of the mining fields, which prompted an auxiliary cycle of revenge killings. The situation was becoming harder to ignore every year, and the violence was spilling out of the up-country and affecting the more touristy areas. Lots of French nationals had begun to come here and Freetown was becoming a French vacation hotspot but the increasing turbulence dashed those hopes. Between tribal blood debt, the corruption and complicity of the local government, and the constantly meddling foreign diamond miners, the situation in Sierra Leone was teetering towards untenability. Situations like we had just encountered with the three guys from California were becoming more common. The loggers family had already gone back to France. His children didn't want to spend their lives here. He felt he would soon be giving it up as he feared civil war would soon come.

He had been running the logging operation with his hired help since his family had left, and it was rumored that he was really hard to work for. I was starting to see both sides. Gigi had learned a lot. He had agreed to help us primarily because he was preparing to leave in what he considered the calm before the storm. He wanted to sell and money was tight, he needed money to be able to take his heavy equipment home. Another contributing factor that can't be understated was that Gigi could pass for French or they would have never spoken in the first place. I told you Gigi was a good pick. The logger found it truly ironic that he would be helping a diamond miner when diamond mining was what was driving him out of this once profitable and peaceful country. Gigi had purchased two five thousand gallon tanker trailers. Each containing about 4 thousand gallons. Additionally, he had arranged their delivery from here to wherever Alusaine wanted them on the other side of the mountain.

Gigi had done a great job. The old logger warned Gigi our days would be numbered and that he better consider it a one-time score. "If you make, take what you make and don't look back, if you get over your head, leave it all and go home," is what he had told Gigi, loosely translated of course.

We got to the village without much trouble. The map was good and the roads had held.

Alusaine was beside himself and happy with the news of the fuel supply. He had been right on the day we first arrived about his feeling. He wanted to give us every assurance that he would mine and collect what he unearthed and that within four weeks, we could return for that payload. We had been there almost 3 weeks; our flight was just two days away now. Alusaine related to me that he had performed a healing ceremony for me upon hearing that I had malaria. I thanked him for his consideration and after finalizing some small details about obtaining the fuel tankers and discussing what had happened over the last few days, we agreed that Mohamed would be our liaison from here to Freetown, and that he would deliver any relevant updates to me when I was back in the States for the next month.

We said our goodbyes and loaded up in the Pathfinder one more time. Surprisingly, Gigi asked Mohamed to drive, to which he agreed.

I believed that we had found a trustworthy friend in Mohamed, and that he would travel up here to ferry information as well as people and things to and from Freetown as required. However, I was not so sure about Alusaine. I was still struggling with the fact that our equipment and tools were being used for anything other than mining, and I felt that I had been made to unwillingly adopt the road out of their village, and that it should have been treated as a completely separate issue from my business with Alusaine. But I decided to be understanding. I understood the necessity of the road, and I was happy to contribute in part. But I felt it would have been more appropriate if in addition to using some of our machinery, they petitioned neighboring villages for help as was their custom—their neighbors also relied on the same road to descend the mountain. Instead Gigi and my investment was shouldering the entire burden.

We had all of Wednesday back at the Mammy Yoko to just wait. That morning, we spent poolside talking and getting a little sun. I looked like a skeleton. I had no scale to weigh myself with, but it was a scary type of skinny. We went to the beach bar for lunch, where once again we had the hummus and flatbread. Gigi said he thought I was gaining weight with every bite. I had slept well the previous night with the expectation that we had all done a great job. I still had to get this parcel of diamonds out, and getting searched was a probability but I somehow knew I wasn't going to let them catch me today. After paying the hotel bill and paying Mohamed, I had about two grand left, which I just put in my front pocket. Also I still had a few hundred dollars in leones. Gigi had done a little shopping during my illness. Mohamed had stopped at a village that was on the way to Alusaine, and there they had purchased 15 or 16 very long snakeskins at roughly twenty dollars apiece. These python skins were once in rare supply, and could fetch upwards of two grand each. This was before pythons became an invasive species in Florida about two decades later. Gigi had called me out into the hotel hallway as we were packing and unrolled one by holding the tail in his hand and throwing the rolled up skin down the hall like a bowling ball. It unfurled into almost a twenty foot perfect hide. My eyebrows practically jumped off my face.

"Are they all this long?" I asked.

"Yeah, most of them."

At any rate, we had to cram a lot of his stuff into my duffel in order for everything to fit. The diamonds were in the money belt, and we were ready to go home.

We decided to take the helicopter to gain some time, even though they didn't have the most impressive safety record. When I first arrived there was a fleet of three and by my last trip they had all crashed. Gigi didn't like the fact that they made you wear inflatable life jackets on the short trip. He had a fear of surviving the crash only to drown by being trapped in the helicopter because of jackets inflating prior to exiting.

Once at Lungi, your baggage is transported for you from the chopper to the terminal, where you still have to go through customs. This customs officer was no different than the rest. He was on the shake down too. I honestly thought that even if he found the diamonds, it was only a matter of how much it was going to cost to let me keep going.

That would likely not be the story on the US side. Even though we had a connecting flight in London again, this time we were not changing airports and our bags had been checked straight through to Miami international.

Once on board the aircraft, it felt so good to be back in the lap of luxury, so to speak. There was one unpleasant little bit before you depart, where they ask passengers to remove their eyeglasses and close their eyes. Some sort of delousing spray is then sprayed on everyone through the air jets above every seat. But as soon as we were airborne, business class was worth every penny. The food, the service, the wide, clean comfortable seats, the pillows, the blankets… You get the idea. It's just that you really miss it after spending three weeks in the bush. You realize that everything you experience is like a miracle of life to those people living in the up-country. A washer and a dryer? Are you kidding? That's the contrast I'm trying to highlight.

We, of course, didn't declare anything of value over ten thousand dollars as we returned. When we collected our bags, Gigi had the bag with the snakeskins, and I had the bag with the dirty laundry. I didn't expect that they would be patting me down for diamonds, so we played a little game, if you will—a little trick. The idea was that Gigi would walk right up to the customs counter, place his bag on it, and open it without being told to do so, and literally hold it half open, while I would act as if I was trying to sneak through in a hurry without being checked. You literally want to try to give the impression that you're up to something nefarious. It worked perfectly— Gigi was waved away without so much as a look inside his half open bag loaded with snakeskin. I was, of course, called back to the counter and asked to open my bag to have my dirty socks inspected. As an extra nice touch, my bag had a locked padlock while his had none. Don't know if they noticed that part but still—flawless entry.

The feeling of getting home for the second time was even better than the first. Especially with the knowledge that if all was going well, I actually had people mining for diamonds on my behalf with tools and equipment I had purchased way up in the up-country right now. That was an indescribable feeling of accomplishment. Mohamed was to call my home number in exactly two weeks to update me on the progress, and in the meantime, I had some diamonds to sell. Life felt like it was firing on all cylinders.

"Oh my God! What happened to you? I can see your bones!" Ygal shooed me away from the entrance of YNG Diamonds with both hands like he was sweeping me out. "Come on, come with me. We will talk about business in a moment, first let's get something to eat."

I followed him to an elevator which took us to the floor that had a cafeteria for the diamond people in the building. We walked up to a door, and Ygal punched in a code to a keypad. The door buzzed and we walked in. Inside the brightly lit cafeteria, there were rows of tables and on one side was the kitchen ordering counter and behind that the stoves and short order cooks. Everyone in the room were Hasidim, wearing traditional clothing, and I was catching some steely looks. We made small talk while we waited at a table for the bagels and cream cheese Ygal had ordered for us by simply holding up two fingers and nodding his head yes.

"This is a private dining room," he explained, as though I couldn't discern that.

Leaning in towards my friend, I whispered, "Ygal, every single person in here is Orthodox, and they aren't exactly being friendly."

I was thinking maybe another eatery would suit us better. His eyes seemed to catch fire suddenly, and contrary to the calm demeanor, I was accustomed to, Ygal practically yelled "These guys? Ehh, don't worry about these guys." Which made me even more uncomfortable. I honestly felt more out of place here than I had in Africa. I finished quickly and waited for Ygal as the sideways glances kept coming.

The Miami sun filtered in through the blinds at YNG Diamonds. Beams of light seemed to highlight the fine layer of dust that inexorably gathers wherever diamond cutters work—it's the residue of microscopic diamond particles that fly off when a stone is worked at the saw. Ygal was mesmerized looking at the parcel of diamonds I had just set before him. He deftly examined the rough stones we had procured in Alusaine's village almost 2 weeks ago. Occasionally, a surprised gasp more than once accompanied by a "*mazel tov*" would escape his otherwise tersely pressed lips, as he sorted them out into little groups for his reference and examined them with critical eyes.

He looked up at me over the rims of his glasses "You managed to do all this?"

"My partner and I did, but not in Freetown. We bought all of these in the up-country."

He pushed his glasses back up the brim of his nose, and leaned back in his leather chair. "Dangerous place. You are either very good or very lucky."

Cracking a smile, I remarked that I'd rather be lucky than good. Ygal wanted the entire lot, and he purchased everything with the exception of one piece of rough that had a very large inclusion in it that fated it for industrial use. I told him that I wanted to have it mounted into a gold setting as a lucky necklace.

"Speaking of industrial stones, what about these?" I asked, fishing around in my right pocket for the wadded up piece of diamond paper that contained the strange triangular pieces the man in the jungle had carried in an animal pelt.

I handed it over to him. He raised an eyebrow in recognition "Ah yes, these are trillions." Trillions. It was the first time I had ever heard the word.

"Are they worth anything?"

"Well, of course, they're diamonds. I don't buy them, but there is a man on the 7th floor, who does."

Ygal rose up out of his seat and stepped towards his wall mounted phone. "I'll call him so he can buzz you in. His name's Jaime."

Ygal and I spoke our farewells and I took the elevator down to the 7th floor. Jaime's office had his name prominently displayed in glazed glass, and I was buzzed in promptly.

"Hello, Ygal sent me to see you. He says you may have an interest in these trillions?"

"I might," came the reply from a rather short and balding man. "Let's have a look."

I passed him the parcel and he took it to a small table behind the counter. It resembled a lab bench to me, and it had a long fluorescent light hanging over it. He began examining the stones and after perusing the trillions, he pivoted back towards me and energetically threw one leg over the bench he was sitting on like one might mount a race horse. "Good quality, super clean!" His face turned to stone suddenly like the excitement coursing through him hit a grounding rod. "Seven-fifty a carat is my absolute top offer. I hope you got them for less than that."

"Slightly." I was convinced that I was presenting a poker face as I nearly spontaneously combusted at the realization of what was happening here.

These trillions were *treasures,* not the industrial waste I was certain they had to be.

"So we have a deal?"

I managed a "Yes" with as much aloofness as possible.

Jaime proceeded to count out eight neat stacks of a thousand dollars in front of me and quickly replaced the space in his safe with the trillions. Between the trillions and what Ygal had purchased, Gigi and I had nearly quadrupled our initial investment. The little cheap bag I had carried since the first trip still served as my money bag, and it was beginning to burst at the seams. I contemplated replacing it as I pinched close the gap between the plastic piping of the bag's zipper and the nylon it was made out of.

I wandered out of the Seybold building in a daze. On the metro rail on my way home back to Kendall, all I could think of was the hide that the poor tribesman had tied around his waist. Somewhere in the up-country jungles outside of Freetown was a man running around barefoot wearing a donated T-Shirt on his back, and unbeknownst to him, he had maybe a half million dollars hanging in the pelt tied to his loop. What a colossal mistake I had made. Why had I not taken them all at twenty-five bucks a stone? They were worth on average about fifteen hundred dollars each back in the States. To this day, when I think of one of the most important opportunities I ever encountered without even really knowing it, I think of his cupped hands overflowing with trillions. A year's study with Ygal had left me ill-prepared for the most fateful meeting yet in the up-country. I knew Gigi was going to have the same reaction as me. So close, we had come so close.

I called Eli and Gigi over to my apartment. They arrived at the same time. I knew Gigi was here before I could see him 'cause I could hear the Chevy. I walked outside to greet them. It was a beautiful day in Kendall. As Eli got out of his car, he stopped before he was even completely out and stared at me.

"Holy shit bro, what happened?"

I knew I had suffered a strong bout of malaria but I thought I was getting back to normal. I didn't realize just how drastic the weight loss had been.

I forgot to mention that my friend Susan's sister and brother-in-law had given me a couch for my apartment. A rather nice one, it was an Egyptian cotton pit couch that formed a curve shape. I had acquired a few sticks of furniture for the apartment, including a coffee table. And now there were rows of bricks there. 38 of them to be precise, on that coffee table. Never before in my life had I counted money by the tens of thousands.

Eli was more or less still fighting against the current and was beginning to fall behind once again on the mortgage payments. He was managing a lot, trying to put his younger brother through college and feed the three of them as well. He was shouldering a heavy load. Gigi was smiling about as big a smile as I had ever seen him smile. I counted the expenses off the top, the entire trip had been free of charge to Gigi, and he had one personal loan to pay back, otherwise he was a lot richer than he'd been since he came to the States. I gave Eli $25K out of my half. He too was beginning to look a little happier. I told Gigi the value of the triangle stones and that they were actually trillions, a valuable type of diamond.

He too instantly recalled the pile we had mostly passed on.

We aren't greedy people, I don't think, we're just practical. Gigi and I began to tell Eli all our experiences.

It was a bit strange returning to rehearsal, but I was happy to be back in the studio. I had enough money to accomplish my original goal, which was one year to work only on the band and a record and all of the different things that entails. I actually could live 3 or 4 years on that much money. But I had the diamond bug. The sky was the limit, and we had an agreement with Alusaine. I couldn't walk away from what we had done and I couldn't wait to get home at night now and check my answering machine for word from Mohamed. We had such a great set-up. The next time should be much easier. The stones would be waiting for us when we arrived to retrieve them. Mohamed would drive Gigi and me up, and we would sit and buy what they had produced for us, and if there was more of an investment to make, we could make it now. I was thinking about what we could do with a crane and a backhoe. The logger and whoever the man was that owned the empty tanker and the crane at a neighboring village were proof that you could get anything up there. Between Gigi and me, we could really build this up by reinvesting the money we each had. We could set ourselves up for a lot longer than a few years. And if we're going to risk our lives anyway, we might as well shoot for a lasting prosperity. I couldn't wait to get home after rehearsal and call Gigi and tell him what I was thinking.

My friend Susan had been driving me to rehearsal for weeks before the last trip one night coming home on highway 826 in a light rain, her old Ford decided to hydroplane and spin in circles. There was no one around us, and eventually, we just hit the dividing wall. Fortunately it was a sideways flat impact and we were actually just able to drive away. The next night she was right back to take me to rehearsal again. I don't forget things like that. So when the time came and I could afford a new car, I didn't get one. Instead I got two used ones. One for her and the other for me. I got her a used but in great shape Riviera. It was a big car with all the bells and whistles and it was a tank that would handle divider walls much better than her old car. It had a red velour interior, not my cup of tea but Susan loved the car. I figured we had bought Mohamed an SUV for $4k, I had to spend at least that for my good friend. I paid $9k for the Riviera and now that I had connections at the Seybold building, I had a custom pair of gold earrings made for her. It was her birthday, and we would be having dinner with her, her best friend, Craig, my guitar player and his wife, Melanie. The four of us went to the Forge Restaurant in Miami to celebrate and that's where I gave her the earrings in appreciation of all of the late night rides to and from the studio. For myself, I purchased a used Ford Mustang 302—it was not the price that mattered here, the dealership was only asking $6k for the white convertible. I loved the way the Mustang sounded and thought that it looked really cool and plus there would be no recurring car payment. I upgraded the stereo system and it was clean. I picked it up with Susan who drove me back to the used lot where they were installing my new stereo. I couldn't wait to get it out on the highway; I pulled onto I95 for the first time, and the Mustang sounded like a race-ready beast. Traffic was light and I decided to push it just a little. I floored it for the first time and the motor literally blew up, with an awful noise of grinding metal parts. I pulled to the side of the road, knowing Susan would be along any second. Long story short, the dealer insisted that the low price was for the 'as is' condition of the car, and would not refund any money. But he said, "If you pay for a rebuilt engine, we will install it free of charge." A factory rebuilt engine was another $2K landed at the dealer's shop, and I guess I should count myself lucky that they had mechanics and a shop to begin with. After about another week, the car was ready. Susan took me once again and this time I drove back to Kendall in a real Mustang 302. I knew I could still love and appreciate the car. I had been home just under two weeks, when finally I received a call from Sierra Leone. It was Mohamed with good news: the fuel had taken a week longer than we agreed because of the now non-stop rain. To the villagers, the rain did not matter, they would dig and wash in almost any conditions, said Mohamed on the phone. "It's so good to hear your voice and I'm glad things are going smoothly." I said, genuinely pleased to hear from him. Mohamed's voice paused with a moment's hesitance "Well, there is one problem. There is an emerging social issue. The young people are tired of living in poverty and there are many demonstrations taking place in the streets. Your fuel is a commodity, and Alusaine has men with guns guarding it. You may be the richest man in Sierra Leone right now, in terms of fuel," he said. I laughed picturing myself that way but he didn't. I realized this was serious, "Alright. Well, we have no choice but to continue under present conditions. Go back and call me when you are sure they have a parcel ready, and I will come right back. We did well with the stones we brought back, and Gigi and I are ready to return as soon as they are ready. Make sure Alusaine is aware of this. I want him motivated."

"Okay Mr. Mark, I will continue to do my level best." A click punctuated his words and a dial tone droned after it. I dialed Gigi to appraise him but got no answer. I left a message on his machine. When the phone rang just seconds after I put it down, I answered, "Hey, Gigi—"

"No, it's Charlie," said the voice on the other end. Charlie was another friend—I could write a whole book about him, but this was at the beginning of our relationship and for the time being, he was the Certified Public Accountant who rented space at the nail salon Susan worked at, and he did taxes and other sometimes more exotic things. He was quickly making himself the go-to guy for just about anything you needed except for drugs. Don't talk to Charlie about drugs. He had just been released from serving 5 years of a 20-year sentence for manslaughter, a charge which had been made worse by the fact that it happened during the commission of a felony. Charlie was transporting a kilo of cocaine across state lines when a drunk pedestrian stepped out in front of his car on a dark road in some state. I didn't need every detail. But he was also selling the python skins we had brought back and the tanners he knew were so happy to get them, he had the coolest snakeskin chaps made for my stage wear along with fingerless gloves also made of snakeskin. The twenty-foot hides were fetching two to three thousand dollars. As I write this today, pythons have become an invasive species and there are pilot programs testing their palatability as a food item.

Charlie had a friend he wanted me to meet. The friend's name was Dave, a Ft Lauderdale fireman and paramedic, who was also a triathlete and an avid skin diver and scuba diver. He had been diving off the reef about a mile offshore and was using a dive flag when a cigarette boat came flying out of somewhere and ran Dave over. When I met with Dave, he told me the story himself, and said he looked down to see what had happened and he could see one of his legs with his fin on it floating to the clear bottom.

I only include this story for one reason, and of course like most occurrences I'm writing about, it can be verified. After I met with Dave, Charlie asked me how I would feel about donating my newly rebuilt 302 Mustang to Dave. He really needed it to be able to pitch his chair in the back and get in with ease. I initially protested, "Charlie, it's not even broken in. I had to replace the engine the first day I had it and I just now got it back."

Undeterred Charlie countered with, "I got fifteen firefighters on board and they each gave a hundred bucks. Come on, Mark, show them you are as good as any 15 firefighters." He slid a slim stack of hundreds into my breast pocket.

"Okay, Charlie, you got it." I felt bad about taking even the $1500. But I was $17k down and still I had no car.

Does no one get the broke musician concept? Charlie has long since moved into his own business and not only is he an accomplished accountant, he also went on to become a pillar of the community and still is, as of this day.

Anyway I brought this up because no good deed goes unpunished. Fast forward to the end of this story, and I see this guy on every channel on the evening news—his name is Gus Machado, and he owns new car dealerships throughout South Florida. He donated a new car to Dave the fireman, who richly deserves it, no doubt, but look at the advertising this guy got. He made it an extravaganza game show atmosphere, with his own name in lights behind him. I hope the reader can see my point here.

The phone rang again, and this time it was Gigi.

"I got your message but we have to talk."

"What's wrong, man? I can tell by your voice something's up."

Gigi's voice modulated up and down in an Italian-esque cadence, even in English.

"It's good actually. It's not bad—nothing is wrong, per se, but Jackie is pregnant."

Jackie was his girlfriend, a very pretty redhead with green eyes. I had only seen her a couple of times with him, and didn't know it was getting serious. Or maybe it happened overnight, no pun intended. I had no idea. But the point was she hadn't been part of the equation, and by the way this was sounding, she was about to be.

"I'm not going to be going back to Africa. I know you are counting on me but I wasn't expecting this, and if I'm going to marry her—

"Wait! What? Marry? Who says you have to get married?" my own voice hit a high note of disbelief that might have been suitable for an operatic drama.

"No, it's my kid. I don't want him born without both parents—a mom and a dad."

"Babies don't know if you're married!"

Clearly his Roman Catholic upbringing in the old country was conflicting with my own values more readily defined by the saints of Los Angeles.

"Yeah I know, but I would know."

"Okay," I relented, "I get it, you're a decent guy, I just hope you love her." My voice trailed off. He tried to sound sincere, which is what gave away that he wasn't, "I do! And I want to take care of them." The last part I believed. "Gigi, look at the money we made. If you're going to be a dad, you're going to need a lot more than that."

Gigi gave a moment's thought to that last point and finally he said, "This money will go a long way. Don't get me wrong, but it wasn't worth the risk. Look at yourself—you still look like a skeleton." He broke the word skeleton into three separate parts unfamiliar with the shape of the word. His cadence picked up attempting to halfway convince me to see things his way.

"Aly said she and her mom ran into you at the mall and you greeted her with a kiss and her mom with a hand shake. They ran to the bathroom to wash their hands as soon as you were done talking."

"Yeah, I did run into them. So what?" I interrupted. "She called me all freaked out that you have AIDs," he pronounced empathically but in a hushed tone. There still was a lot of stigma around AIDs at that time, and a lot of fear about its transmissibility. "I had to tell them you didn't get AIDs in Africa; you got malaria. But do you see my point?"

"No I don't." And I really didn't.

Gigi continued, "You almost did die, and you could have, and Nelson did die and the guys from California did die."

There it was. I knew it. I knew it was weird that we never spoke of the man and his two deceased companions at the logging camp. We hadn't let it deter us in the least. And I have to agree that was weird behavior on our part. But here it was, and I couldn't deny what he was saying.

I tried to counter with, "What about the part where you never felt more alive in your life than when you were tearing up the road in an old Benz?"

"Yeah, it's true" he admitted "But that doesn't mean it's not crazy. I have to think like a stable 30-year-old now, and I can't leave my job for the better part of the month. And the whole thing is a gamble to begin with."

I could follow his logic but I can't stress enough how Gigi was the only person I trusted to brave the up-country with me. I needed someone I could trust to watch my back now more than ever with unrest brewing. You can't just put an ad in the newspaper looking for a jungle fighter.

"Fuck man, this puts me in a spot, Gigi. There's no one else I can rely on out there! There's no one else that could take it! No offense, but can you imagine any of the guys in the band in the up-country, without their hairspray? Eli would not take a shit the whole time he was there just so he didn't have to wipe his ass in the woods and bury his own shit. Come on, buddy, it takes a special guy to bury his own shit. I need you," I implored in a last ditch effort to sway Gigi from a reasonable path.

"No man, I'm serious. And Dennis would fire me. I'm practically running the place as it is."

I was just listening at this point. "You can keep my part of the investment for the work we did over there, maybe just one favor—get me a good deal on a cut stone from Ygal.

"Sure thing," I said. "And hey, congratulations on both the wedding and the child. You're going to be a good dad."

Things were starting to go a little sideways on me, and here I was, again on my own in this thing.

I thought I should go to the doctor and get checked out. I set an appointment with a doctor I found in the phone book, a Doctor Quintana, a Puerto Rican guy. He did some blood work and I remember his name because it required several visits. I had suffered a bad case of malaria but also now I had built up antibodies—that was the good news. The bad news is that once you have it, you have it forever. So consider that if you ever attempt to do this.

It had now been about two weeks since I had heard from Mohamed. I went online one night after rehearsal and got a state advisory for Sierra Leone. A travel advisory had been issued to avoid all travel there. Travel only if absolutely necessary, it said. Violence had been reported to be occurring at checkpoints.

It was feeling a little lonely. The band wasn't into the Africa stuff, and they all had their own lives. Gigi was no longer involved—he had his own life. Eli had become my confidant but there was no way he could go. He had caught up on the mortgage, and had some months in front of him to work with. Twenty five grand used to go a lot further in the early 90s.

I decided to wait out the couple of months still left in the rainy season— no reason to even attempt anything until it passes. In the meantime, we had sold out a club called the Button South on usually dead Thursday nights and then we did it again, and pretty soon, we were opening for a lot of national acts. But we still had no record deal. Our manager at the time had a friend who was managing a band called Marilyn Manson and the Spooky Kids. And he asked if she would let them open for us on one of those Thursdays, he would owe her a favor blah blah. That kid was a trip. They didn't even have a drummer but he had this villainous persona and this androgynous stage presence that he sold well; it was interesting. Also a few other things of that nature were going on. Life was still mostly on the up. One effect the money had was that rehearsals were much less stressful, especially when you don't have to think about groceries, light bill, rent etc. I was still holding out on buying my own car, and Susan was still driving me. I needed to have as much of that money available if the opportunity came up, and if not, I had to keep stretching it out. I didn't know what was coming next. I just knew I hadn't given up. I was hitting the gym mostly for cardio. You could say I was training so that in the event I should have to run for my life, I would be able to. I had gained all the normal weight back that I needed to not look like I was dying of a virus. In fact, I was getting in not so bad shape. We got offered a little money to do a five song CD, which we gladly took and did. The CD is titled *Mr. Red, White, Blue,* and of course, you can probably find it on YouTube now. Along with a few videos that we did for a second full length CD titled *You Can't Bargain with God*. Some of you might even remember the song *One Summer Night;* it played all over the country. That was our song. I guess I had accomplished what I wanted to accomplish as the band and the spurt in popularity were all reason enough to call it a career and pursue it. But still almost $40k worth of stuff sitting in the jungle? I had to at least get back there and take a look, shouldn't I?

The phone rang on a Saturday afternoon in Kendall. It was Mohamed. His voice was shaky, "Hello, Mr. Mark."

"I knew you'd call. I knew I could count on you. How are you?"

"I am not so well, Mr. Mark. Those bastards took my arm."

I could hear him speaking through gritted teeth. "Who? Who took your, did you say, arm?"

My mind was spinning as I tried to appraise the situation unfolding three thousand miles across the ocean that was turning into something surreal.

"Yes, it's those bastards, RUF, they hold me down and they ask 'you want long sleeve or short sleeve?' and they cut my arm off with a machete."

I was stunned—Mohamed had been made an amputee in an act of senseless violence. I asked him if there was anything I could do to help.

"I'm calling you because you were a nice person and I believed you would go far here. Not everyone is like you, but you are a true person. But also I am taking the Pathfinder and I am leaving with my wife and daughter. I will not be here to meet you or to drive you. You should think about forgetting about the up-country. These kids, they don't respect nothing, they ain't going to respect you either. They only respect the drugs now."

I sat down and sank into the Egyptian couch next to the phone. I expressed my remorse for what had happened to him and thanked him for calling me to let me know. He could have understandably just disappeared.

"Please forgive me. You were an honorable partner," Mohamed replied.

I shook my head reflexively though of course Mohamed could not see that.

"No, that's crazy—what you're telling me. That's a very harsh reality. I get it, you are going to do what you have to do, how are you getting out of the country?"

"I'm traveling by the same side of that mountain that you get the fuel from," he said, "I'm also going to use some of your fuel."

"Mohamed, are you in pain?" I asked.

"No," he said. "It does not hurt anymore. I found some pain drug but I can still feel it like it is there sometimes."

What a harsh and strange reality. I was sitting poolside in South Florida and going out to dinner, going to rehearsal, and at this point, we were working in a nice studio and at the same time the guy on the other end of this line was living in a type of desperation most of us will never even think of. They cut his arm off because they wanted to make a statement. And their statement was 'it's our turn, get out or we may kill you next time'. There is no recourse there. There's no one to complain to; there is no way to seek compensation, no police to come take a report, no lawyers to sue on your behalf. Hell, there isn't even anyone there who can stop them from hurting you. No Gus Machado car giveaway for your lost limbs here.

"I'm sorry, Mohamed, if you get to some place where I can send you money, call me back. Tell your wife and daughter I wish I could have met them. Thank you for your help. I always believed you could go far too."

"Thank you, my friend," was all he said and the line disconnected.

I hadn't thought to ask him a number of things. I just kept thinking of his reality versus mine. But now I wish I had just thought to ask if Alusaine knew. At any rate, I knew what road he would be on for his trip and he would have to stop at Alusaine's village to get gas. He had said as much. That night on the evening news, there was a small mention of the UN increasing its ground presence in Freetown to quell civil unrest, after government officials had said that without their help, their own forces would be insufficient to adequately respond to the rise in violence that was occurring all over the country.

Three weeks had passed since I had last heard from Mohamed. We were in fall here, which meant the rainy season would be over in Sierra Leone. I checked the mail and was surprised to find a letter from Alusaine. In it he explained that the fuel had arrived but two weeks later, it had been the center of a minor skirmish between RUF rebels and village miners. Possession of my fuel tanker had changed hands apparently several times. Alusaine said the tanker was too heavy to move without a half-track but the rebels had been filling large yellow plastic containers that they could carry by hand. His fear, he had continued, was that soon the RUF forces would be large enough in numbers to overturn entire villages, which would of course give them control of the mining fields. They were very busy recruiting and they were being supplied with a lot of dope, crystal meth, cocaine and hypodermic needles. Someone had an interest in seeing a revolution, it seemed. And there were already rumors of RUF child fighters entering smaller villages, where they could overpower the men and women, and cut off their arms. I know they got Mohamed in Freetown. When we spoke, he said that no one even tried to stop them—it was in the middle of the day, and no one did anything to the little pissants. Even though Alusaine had encountered some trouble with the newly stirring rebellion he said that he had diamonds for me to come and buy and that was all that really counted. Alusaine and the elders certainly were not throwing in the towel and giving up their land. The truth was that even though it was very slow, from year to year, growth did occur in the villages, a well would spring up in one village center and perhaps in another a new school building would be built, and still in another, a pavilion to shade the people who gather there would come up. And for almost twenty years, this had gone on, mostly in peace. There were always going to be exceptions. However, the increase in violence and robbery being perpetrated on mining villages was on the increase, and there had been armed skirmishes for this piece or that field beginning to occur more frequently. I decided it still felt safe enough to go. But the intent behind the words of the French logger and what he had told Gigi he expected were also on my mind.

Things were continuing to happen with FarrCry, the *Mr. Red White Blue* CD had gone into record stores like Peaches and Sam's, and had sold about seven thousand copies. So that had generated a little more buzz for the band. Lory Hibbard had come to a sound check and interviewed Craig the guitar player and myself, for her television show, *The Buzz*. It felt cool to be at home getting ready to go to rehearsal with the news on and hear Rick Sanchez introduce the segment. And that had kept me busy and happy about it too. So did I really need to go back and risk everything again?

· It only took me two days to decide that yes, I had to go back. You could say I was a motivated person, but I would tell you that it was fear that was the great motivator. I was 8 years older than Eli, who was the closest to me in age. I was ten years older than the other 3. So I was the old man for sure. I was going on 31 and I was already quite sure that there were no guarantees in life. I knew the odds of "making it" were astronomical. And they were. But it was all about how you defined "making it".

To me, someone who had been playing in bars starting with bottle clubs when I was 16 the musical lifestyle was the lifestyle I had come to love. The band was your family and there was no better place to be, than on the road with your family. So if I could do this for free, I would. There was this little band that played at a hotel I had a job at when I was 15—the job was like a bellboy/'run and get whatever anyone tells you to' type of gig. But there was this band there, a house band, blues trio, black guys and I would hear them and sometimes watch them rehearse in the early afternoon when they woke up. And I knew they would play till one or two in the morning and go up to their rooms and party every night. And when I would come to work in the mornings around 11, I would have to pick up all of their room service plates, and there was always a whiskey bottle and roaches in the ashtray. And I remember thinking that was truly the life I wanted; I wanted to be them. You might think it's strange what I just said, but it's the feeling that their mess evoked, like some sort of *déjà vu*. I really hope that makes sense to someone. The point is I wanted to assure myself that I could afford that lifestyle for the rest of my life without it ever being contingent on "making it" and if that's not love and dedication then I don't know what is.

I suppose the proof is in the pudding, as they say—I'm still writing songs and making records today.

CHAPTER 8

I kept thinking of Alusaine and wondering how things were progressing with the RUF altercations. I went online frequently to see if there were any updates. And the only one I had seen definitely advised against traveling and said many checkpoints were closed

I tried calling the Mammy Yoko but there was a constant busy signal. But as fate would have it, the situation was about to start showing promise. Three more weeks had passed. I was able to book a flight to Sierra Leone, but every attempt at booking a room ended in a frustrating busy signal. So I thought the decision was made for me, at this point. Because without a place to stay, and there were no rental cars to be had, and I wouldn't have a place to land. I was home from rehearsal again on this particular night. I hadn't been home long—it was 2 am when the phone rang. I answered thinking it was probably someone from the band, but it was not.

The voice on the other end sounded all at once British but not British. I couldn't place it. He said his name was Max Hasheem, and he was given my telephone number by Alusaine. "I am in Freetown presently but I live in Kangbe, right on the outskirts where I have a house. I wanted to introduce myself—it seems we are neighbors, in a way".

"Oh, how so?"

"In Kamalu," he replied. "I have a parcel close to that village."

I didn't want to admit that I hadn't actually known the name of Alusaine's village. It's not like there are street signs, or streets, for that matter. Alusaine's letter had to be mailed from Freetown. There wasn't even postal service in the up-country. I pretended I did though by just simply going along with him.

"Oh yes, yes, of course, Mr. Shaheem. I've even been by your place," I told him. "I saw it from a distance of course, but you have a crane and a fuel tanker up there. I had to see that for myself. Pleasure to meet you, sir."

"Likewise, I'm so sorry to have awakened you at this hour," he said. "It's just gone past nine in the morning here and I had to take the opportunity to use the telephone while they're operational again."

"No, not a problem," I assured him. "I actually am a night person so I was still up and wide awake".

"Oh, that's lovely. Have you got a moment to discuss a little business then?"

"Yes, of course."

"I'll go straight to the point," he said. "I like your intentions and I admire that you got as far as you've gotten. I understand you somehow got a fuel tanker to Kamalu yourself."

"I did, well, with the help of my partner, but yes," I responded.

"Oh, so you have a partner?" he asked.

"Yes or at least I had a partner. It was more of a one-time thing with him. He was only ever going to help me set up a light flow of rough out of the village, just a one-man operation. I was just trying to book a reservation at the Mammy Yoko so that I could book a flight but it's an endless busy signal."

"Yes. But that's not a telephone issue. The hotels in town are closed. They are very worried about the RUF and until the UN says that they have everything back under control, they will remain closed. These little heathens are disrupting everything, but they are not in control. They are mostly children, but the drugs and the brainwashing are making them more vicious than any adult soldier I've ever seen… But take heart, all is not lost, you could stay with us when you come. I was hoping we could be of assistance to each other."

"Ok, I'm listening, what did you have in mind?"

So we talked about his need for heavy equipment, the crane that was presently on site was not just out of fuel, they had blown a something or other and the bottom line was that the crane that was there would never dig again.

"It is broken beyond repair," he lamented.

Essentially Max explained that they had everything they needed, with the exception of earth moving machines, to mine that parcel. They were seeking partners who basically had the clout to buy or lease these machines for them, and have them land in Freetown. From there, Max said he had all the experience necessary to move heavy equipment to the up-country. He was originally from Egypt but studied in London, he told me, explaining the mixed accent with which he spoke. I took him up on his offer to stay at his home while the hotels were closed.

I told Eli what was going on and about the call. He was very skeptical, of course. We hadn't really discussed what was in it for us at all. I said, "Eli, even if we can't do what he's asking, I can at least go back up-country to purchase what they have mined since we equipped them.

And if there is something we can get involved in, we'll do our best. I'm not exactly broke and don't forget, the place has been good to us. And Alusaine's letter says he has something for us. Let's finish what we started. "

Look at it like one of those timeshare pitches, free trip if you attend our sales pitch and then you get two lovely nights on us just for listening".

At least that made him laugh. "So what's my part exactly?" Eli asked.

"You are just my really cool entrepreneur Miami friend. And if I call you, just act like you have to approve everything, ask me questions, things of that nature," I explained.

"And what will that accomplish?" he persisted.

"Appearances" I said. "I don't want them to think I'm out there alone. So if I call, just play along, you'll get it, if and when the time comes."

"Okay, okay, I get ya. How are you getting to the airport?" he asked.

I just smiled at him, it took him a second, but he realized. "Oh, me. Okay, okay, I still got ya."

I was bringing $50k with me this time, and I was leaving the rest in hiding places in the apartment. I had stashed money in toaster strudel boxes in the freezer, in the air vents, in plastic bags stuffed inside the Egyptian sofa. I hid a key in the restroom of the pool right across the parking spots intended for my building. If I needed access to the money I could call Gigi and tell him where the key was. I would listen to Max's sales pitch and use his place as my base, he had to take me by Alusaine's in order to get to his parcel anyway. This was most fortuitous, I thought. The worst case scenario I could envision was that I might actually be able to help them with their need for caterpillar parts and or John Deere equipment. He could be a place for me to land while there were no hotels; he could maybe even keep an eye on his neighbors in the up-country. This could be a very good thing. For now, Max was seeing me as a guy who could just jet back to Africa at a moment's notice, all it took was an invite. I wanted to keep that appearance for the time being.

The flight times had changed and now there was only one flight every two weeks on KLM. The connections had changed as well. And on the second leg of the trip, we had a stopover in Morocco. As we taxied on the tarmac, the pilot came on over the intercom and said words to the effect of, "Ladies and gentlemen, we will be making a brief stop for passengers. As we approach, please make sure to keep the window shades closed and remember photography is not allowed, and for any Americans bold enough to be deplaning, please remember no photography is allowed inside the airport either." I was sitting with headphones on in business class listening to *Black Cat* on the in-flight entertainment system again. Next stop would be Lungi airport.

We arrived at Lungi much later in the night we had when we visited earlier. It was almost midnight local time when I stepped onto the tarmac again. I walked towards the terminal building. There wasn't the usual hubbub of people packed in there. In fact, it was pretty quiet and as I looked around behind me, only about half a dozen people had gotten off the flight here, sitting near the front of the plane, deep in thought and listening to music I had not noticed that most of coach had gotten off the flight in Morocco. I made my way into the building and collected my duffle from a small pile right in front of customs. There was no customs officer, no one to check the contents of your bag. It was a bit disconcerting. I walked past the customs tables towards the curb and there was a man with blue jeans and a blue button-down shirt, black high top converse shoes. He was short, I had pictured him as tall and dark-skinned, I was half-right. He had a full head of thick, black hair, and a bushy mustache. This particular night he had a red bandanna tied cowboy style around his neck.

"Mr. Christian," He voiced in an exaggerated and stern British accent trailing into a huge pregnant pause. Had he just done Captain Bligh?

He broke into mirthful laughter, "I love that movie," he said extending his hand. He had done Captain Bligh!

We shook hands, "Pleasure to meet you in person."

He gave a firm but not Napoleon-complex-firm hand shake, and skipped over the duffle bag I had just set down, and bent to pick it up.

"I've got this," he said. Making the usual small talk, he said, "You must be tired. Your journey began yesterday. How many hours did it take?"

"About 35 hours. We had an unusual stop in Morocco."

He walked with a bit of a bounce and a sense of purpose. He seemed energetic and spry for a man of about 50. He walked to a pretty nice Toyota land cruiser.

"We're taking the ferry, I assume?"

"Yes," he nodded towards a black land cruiser ahead of us. "This is us. And we'll have no choice but the ferry I'm afraid," he grunted, throwing our bags into the back of the land cruiser.

"Why's that?"

"The last helicopter crashed three of three in the fleet—all crashed. The last one unfortunately over land, with no survivors." Gigi and I had flown on that last helicopter.

Again there was not much traffic on the ferry—this was the last trip of the day. We continued to make small talk as we drove back off the ferry and through the now empty streets of Freetown. There was no electricity, no trash can fires. It was about quarter to one. We drove past the beach road, which would have taken us to the hotels. He headed through an area that I had seen before on the way to the up-country. There was a peninsula and on it, there was a beach, and on the beach, was a big two-story house. You could see it from the main road through town. I had wondered whose home it might be. And now we were headed there. The house was lit up and was the only place with electricity in sight. You could see the house from the beach side easily but the front entrance of the house was an eight foot wall, with a large wooden gate that rolled on a track against the wall to open. There was razor wire lining the tops of the three walls that made up the front entrance. On the beach side, there was no wall, just a beautiful view of the ocean and the inlet. The gate opened as we approached but it was not automatic—someone had been waiting for us to return. We rolled towards the open gate and Max turned towards me in the passenger seat and said, "Welcome to my home." We drove into the courtyard and the gate was pushed closed behind us and locked by a giant of a man called Tamba. After he finished with the gate, he walked towards us and Max introduced himself. We shook hands, and his hand made mine look like a tiny doll hand in comparison. "He's our security officer," Max said. It was then that I noticed that Tamba's khaki shorts and the khaki shirt were part of an army uniform. I grabbed my duffle from the back seat, and Tamba said, "Let me take that for you. I will place it in the room which you will be using."

I thanked him and then I followed them up a narrow concrete set of steps that were outside of the building and not under cover. They led up to an entrance that took you into the home by way of a kitchen. But you passed out of the kitchen into a large living room and dining room area and off of that living area were two double wide French doors that were currently open. The air had a slight chill and you could smell the ocean. The room had a nice ambience. There was a man there waiting for us. He was a tall Dutch man with blond hair and blue eyes. He spoke English but just barely, he too was in his fifties. I introduced myself just because of my proximity and learned his name was Jan. Max was now behind me. And Tamba disappeared out the open French doors. There was an awkward moment or two as the three of us now stood there looking at each other. Max did what almost all humans all over the free world seem to do. They go to play. "Who wants a drink, we have Scotch and Scotch." Max seemed like he was a bit of a joker. "I would just like a coke if we happen to have one," I said. Jan nodded yes to a Scotch.

I asked where my room was as I needed to retrieve something from my luggage. Tamba, who was now back in the doorway, pointed to his left, and said, "This way Mr. Mark."

"Excuse me for just a few moments," I said.

Max had his attention on the Scotch glasses he was preparing. "Certainly, take your time you may want to wash up. Are you hungry?" Max asked, and at the same time managed to shoot a glance at me without spilling a drop of the Scotch he was pouring into the second glass.

"No, thank you, the in-flight menu on KLM was excellent. And I had dinner maybe two hours ago."

I went into my room—it was very simple, and had a bed, one dresser with a mirror and that was it. It did have its own bathroom, which was a nice touch. I washed up a bit and toweled off, and I opened my duffle bag and from it I took the John Deere catalog and the lease forms I had acquired back in South Florida. In my head, I had formulated another plan. I was hoping it wouldn't backfire like trying to pose as a diamond buyer with a credit card had done. Maybe I had learned a lesson. Just remembering to be careful of such things was proof that I may have.

When I returned, the mood seemed light and comfortable. The three men were sitting in the living room, a bowl of fruit had been set out, and the Scotch seemed to have Max and Jan relaxed and in a jovial mood. The three of them were laughing at a joke one of them had told. There was an open seat just next to the sofa the two men were sitting on, and Tamba occupied the seat on the other end. Just as I sat down, Tamba's eyes drifted towards the open French doors. "Mariama is here," he said, and simultaneously Max and Jan began to chatter at our guest excitedly. I looked up expecting a person but instead saw a chimpanzee, about the size of a two-year-old child, deftly swinging in over the veranda into the living room sailing over the furniture and landing near the bowl of fruit where she helped herself to its contents. Obviously, the chimpanzee had been here before. The name they had given her 'Mariama' meant 'gift from God'. Unfortunately, I thought the fact that this chimp was here meant that others had died—there was a trade in chimpanzee hands and other parts, and this youngster was probably separated from its troop by the lowlife poachers who dealt in such things. We had bought and traded in snakeskin, but to me, there was a huge difference, and the snakes were not endangered, if anything, they posed a danger to cattle and goats and such. It may sound like a justification, but that's only because it is.

"Just be careful, she's a sweetheart as long as she doesn't feel threatened," they warned.

Just then she arrived at the back of my chair in one graceful movement from the table. She held out her hand palm down, so I slowly did the same thing, she suddenly dropped her extended hand and grabbed my pony tail with the other. "She wants to know you," Jan said. "She did the same thing to me when I arrived." Mariama was now sniffing my hair. Suddenly, she released it and as soon as it had started the inspection was done, and she was back at the fruit.

"Okay, now you are part of the troop too. She accepts you. Let's talk about diamonds," Max said, as he poured another drink for himself and one for Jan. I couldn't tell if he was serious about the troop comment. This guy was a bit of a card.

We had gotten down to talking about diamonds and the up-country, we covered a lot of topics, and I was honest with all my answers to his questions about the things we had done and the parcels I had bought since I've been coming here. He didn't seem at all convinced that we had bought fuel from the loggers and had it delivered to miners. "That Jean Pierre is a total cock-wombel," Max said. "I'm pretty sure the last thing he would do is sell fuel to an American diamond smuggler. I would bet any price on that." I explained to the both of them that my partner Gigi was one of the French loggers' countrymen, and he had taken a liking to Gigi and had let us stay the night.

This seemed to calm his suspicion, and I felt it was good he would see that if he were honest with me, I would be very honest with him.

I had an angle and I even so much as explained it to him. If he could transport me back to Kamalu so I could meet with Alusaine and the sellers, and if he could from his own parcel produce anything that would impress my boss Eli back at home, we might be able to pick a couple of earth movers out of this catalog and have him sign this lease when I go home.

"Has he got that kind of money? Your boss, I mean."

I took a swig of coke out of the glass in front of me, and said, "Absolutely, he's a venture capitalist. There are a lot of loose ends still of course, what would the split be and such things, he may also have other questions or stipulations, as I'm sure the both of you do."

Max nodded encouragingly and I added, "But let's start from the beginning and show me what we're working with."

Max glanced at the bottle of Scotch in the center of the table but decided against refreshing his quarter full glass, and said, "Well, you are already quite aware of the inner workings as you have equipment here yourself, and you have seen the up-country."

The Egyptian paused for a moment and clicked his teeth as he thought of a question. "Have you also brought money to pay the miners?"

"Yes, some, and if I need more, I can probably get it."

"Okay, then!" Max said, clapping his hands together once. "Then it's settled, we will leave for the up-country tomorrow, just you, Tamba and I. Jan is staying here to keep an eye on things." Max tossed back the remainder of his drink and closed our meeting, saying, "We have a long day tomorrow. I'm going to bed." We all agreed and said goodnight. Mariama was back on the veranda nibbling on a piece of fruit.

"We leave the beach doors open; we have armed guards downstairs outside—they are out there all night," Max said peeking out at Mariama.

"I'll have them turn off the generator in fifteen minutes if that's suitable," interjected Tamba. "Thank you, my good man." Max responded

I went back to my room and closed the door. I got ready for bed and as I was reaching to turn out my light, it went off. I hadn't noticed the hum of the generator until it stopped. It was very quiet, and all I could hear was the jungle sounds I was now familiar with. We were back in Africa. I stared up at the popcorned ceiling thinking to myself 'You crazy fucker!'

I must have been tired. I slept well into daylight. I'm not sure what time it actually was or what woke me up. Maybe it was the smell of coffee brewing. I grabbed a T-shirt from my bag, and put on jeans and work boots, and walked out onto the open porch, where I had last seen Mariama sitting and eating fruit. But there was no mess of any kind. The living room area was clean too. As I walked towards the smell of the coffee, I heard voices. The coffee pot was in the kitchen by the window and as I looked for a cup, I happened to glance through the window and I saw Pauline standing by the passenger side of a running car. I thought that was an odd coincidence. I stepped out onto the concrete stairway and looked down at her. She saw me and the nervousness was palpable even from the top of the stairs.

In Africa, someone is always watching. Someone had alerted Pauline. This meant that somehow even in the middle of the night between here and the tarmac, someone was watching. I made my way downstairs.

"You look a little nervous Pauline," I said briskly. "Surprised to see me again?"

"Mr. Mark, let me have a word with you please," she said. But Max was coming from some place downstairs under the main floor, even though I had seen no staircase inside. Perhaps it was a garage. Max had two armed men following him and he interrupted before I could speak. "We have a long drive today and it's past ten already. I'm sorry but we have no time." Max said, speaking sternly.

A Muslim gentleman emerged from the same area, and he walked quickly to the car and got in, Pauline was back in the passenger seat shaking her hands at the driver as she began to speak to him immediately even as he was getting into the car. He was shaking his head vigorously no. As if in an argument, they backed out of the compound and the two guards closed the gate behind them.

"What was she doing here?" I asked Max.

"Let's go back up to the kitchen and have some coffee," Max responded. I began to protest.

"I'll tell you over coffee," he insisted.

Back in the kitchen, Max said, "That woman is bad news. She worked in the hotel before they boarded up."

"I'm aware of that, Max," I said. "I'm 99 percent sure her and her husband had me set up"

"You can be 100 percent sure," Max replied. "You got away with your money, your life and most impressive of all, with one of the, if not the best stone in the parcel, for much less than it was worth. The robbers you were dealing with didn't think you would not be back and they were indeed trying to bait you back. You were supposed to see that diamond in the light with your loupe and think that they all must be that good, which they weren't, but when you returned you would have been robbed and killed and discarded in the common way. You burned them for about 20 thousand guilders. They were very angry that you got away, so they took retribution on her husband. I bet you were in a lot of trouble when you were a lad, Mr. Christian."

"But why was she here?" I asked. "She works at the airport now. She saw us leaving last night. Everyone knows who lives at the big house on the peninsula and drives the black land cruiser. Those men that tried to rob you broke both of her husband's arms so that his wife would have to wipe his ass. He was in a cast for 3 months, but it didn't stop there. They are holding them both responsible for the twenty thousand guilders. Pauline got here first thing this morning. She told me the story and was begging me to convince you that she had no idea they were going to rob you and plead for you to help them somehow."

Max looked at me momentarily judging my response. I shrugged. "They made their bed, Max, as far as I'm concerned, they can continue to sleep in it."

"Exactly," he agreed, stabbing a finger at the air. "I knew that she knew about the set-up, I could just tell when she was telling me the story something was off."

Max nodded up at me with his chin quizzically. "How did you know they were going to rob you? What made you escape?"

"The same way you knew Pauline was lying."

"The car is packed and ready, the generator fuel is in the back, and everything here is secure, sir," Tamba recited in a military checklist fashion to Max.

"Are you ready to head up–country, Mr. Christian?" Tamba's deep eyes regarded me matter-of-factly.

"Let me grab my bag," I replied, glad that I was completely ready to depart. Max raised a finger in the air. "Oh, would you mind leaving the catalogs here for Jan?"

I shook my head. "No, of course not. That's why they are here. Have him study what he wants and let's see if you and I can make it happen." I jogged off up the stairs towards my room.

The Land Cruiser was newer and in much better shape than the Pathfinder. It too had reinforced undercarriage and the elevated exhaust. We left probably just before noon, maybe closer to eleven, as we pulled out of the compound for the first time. The streets were completely empty. Compared to what they were usually like, they were bare, maybe a pedestrian here a bicycle over there, but it was a stark, stark contrast. Where had nearly one million people gone? As we turned off the peninsula back on the main road into town, I noticed an Alcoholics Anonymous symbol—it was painted on a wall that was better seen when coming from the airport. It was large, maybe 15 feet in circumference. How had I not noticed it before? We were now passing through the area that the large outside market I had walked through on the first trip was in. I remembered the chimpanzee hands fashioned into ashtrays, and I thought of the friendly, smart, curious creature I had met last night. The place where all the pelts were was also closed. I was happy about that in a strange way. I know it didn't mean that the poachers were gone, but at least they had been forced to stop for a while. I said to Max, "This is a little scary, where is everyone?" The capital city had truly become a ghost town.

"They are all in hiding, some people have fled into Guinea, some into the mountains." Max continued, "They are very scared that civil war is coming."

We were passing the turn off that would take us right to the Mammy Yoko. I asked Max if he would mind stopping. I just wanted to see it and maybe take a few photos with the camera I had brought with me. He asked Tamba if he thought it was safe. "Perhaps if we don't stay too long, it is okay." Max shrugged and took the turn towards the hotel.

The place looked unrecognizable. It had been all boarded up. The fountain in front was now empty and the vegetation around it dead. In the space of a few months, it had withered into a shell. I took photos, and headed around the back just to have a look. Tamba shouted to me to wait for him which I did, and I turned to see him coming with a Russian-type assault weapon, a Kalashnikov I believe, slung over his shoulder. The sense of dread in Freetown became palpable for me at that moment, and Jim Morrison lyrics sprung to mind, '*The future's uncertain and the end is always near.*'

I got about halfway around the building and I had seen enough. The ground was littered with dirtied syringes and dotted with little plastic bags by the thousands. Who was supplying the needles? World Health Organization? Red Cross? Or were they being rationed? Was it the same factions that were providing the guns and the bullets?

I came back to the truck winding the exposed film in the camera so I could remove the cartridge and replace it with a new roll. When an ECOMOG and a UN truck came up on us rather quickly. A blue helmet exited the UN truck from the passenger side and began speaking loudly. "This area is closed. No further photography is permitted, and please be so kind as to give to me the roll you were putting away when we arrived."

I noticed he was wearing army fatigues in place of the blue jumpsuit I had seen when disasters struck other parts of the world. "Don't argue with them, Mark," Max said.

I took the roll back out of the camera bag and handed it to him. By that time, a white helmet had also come up. "Was that the only roll you have taken?" asked the white helmet. "It wasn't a whole roll; there were other photos on that roll, I just took a few and that filled the roll," I explained.

"What is your purpose here?" demanded the white helmet.

"I've been a guest here a couple of times and I just wanted to see it again."

That seemed to satisfy his curiosity and he scorned us all. "The sign says 'Closed,' gentlemen," he pointed above his head towards the posted notice. "Move along now and don't be coming back for any more photos." He nodded at the blue helmet, who was walking back to his vehicle, and we got out of there. "That was relatively easy," I said to both of them.

"No, that was close," Max said. "If they start asking for papers and passports and questioning us, we could be here all day. What did you need the photos for anyways?"

"Just keeping a record for my boss. Every little thing helps. With those photos, for example, I can show Eli my boss, how useful it is to have you here since we would have no place to stay as this is the condition of the hotel."

Max wiggled his jaw unsatisfied with my apparent obtuseness.

"I want the partnership with you to work, Max, so I'm going to highlight value wherever I can in an attempt to convince him to lease the machines for us and ship them here. That's why it's important that Alusaine have something good for me to purchase. I want to prove that the last time was not a one-off or a fluke," I said, and continued, "I need to have something from you that will further convince him. He's already aware that we couldn't be making this scheduled trip without your help, so we're off to a good start."

As we got to about the halfway point of the trip, we stopped at a village for some coconut water. Coconuts were chilled in the river and opened by chopping a hole on the top. Usually a straw would then be inserted, but there were no straws available so we put the hole in the coconuts and drank 'em bottom up.

It was then that I realized that Max had been in the up-country for a while. More than once a passerby would yell to Max, "Hey, Padi how da body"? And Max would respond in Krio, "Da body fine I tenkgod."

He was known at every checkpoint, and if he wasn't immediately recognized, he knew enough names and enough Krio to talk his way right past. He seemed to enjoy the recognition and he seemed to really like the people. That seemed to be a common thread among foreigners that were accepted around here. Maybe I too would continue to come back if things went well. Stranger things had happened. We drank our coconut water and got back in the truck. With the roads fixed, and the parts that couldn't be fixed ingeniously rerouted, we would reach our destination before nightfall.

Once again I had spoken too soon, there was still a part of the road that they had not managed to fix or reroute. It was a pretty damaged area as there was a deep, muddy hole, which had only gotten worse with vehicles attempting to cross it. Max entered the muddy pit slowly and right away the four wheel drive was struggling to find a grip on the road. We began hitting submerged tree branches and holes within the hole that we just couldn't see. The truck bottomed hard a couple of times but it kept running. At one point, we had become balanced in a weird and awkward way, the truck was resting on a log or a mud bar but we couldn't go forward or backward. Both Tamba and I had to get out and stand on the rear bumper to try to weigh it down enough for the rear tires to get a grip on something and push itself over that tipping point. We started bouncing on the rear and I began to count to three on the downward thrust just for rhythm and so Max could time his use of the gas pedal. On one of those counts Max had gunned it just right and the land cruiser launched itself almost straight up, leaving Tamba and I to fall on our butts in the mud. Fortunately, the truck came down just over the unseen ledge it had been teetering over, and we were able to keep crawling along, we eventually made it through that section of the road, but it had taken probably close to an hour. It gets dark early in December there, so we passed Alusaine's village after sunset. Max's truck was known to people in that village, so if there had been anyone on watch at the village perimeter, they would have probably seen us.

We didn't have to travel terribly far past Alusaine's village. Even as we ambled slowly around the mountain in the darkness, I could tell that Gigi and I had traveled on or near this way when we were searching for the path to the logging camp. The fields that Max was working near were also butted up against directly by diamond fields that belonged to other villages. This created a kind of co-opt of miners. As far as I could tell, Max was the only foreigner up here partnered with a village besides me. Everyone else mining the fields was a native. Fires blazing in empty oil drums loosely demarcated Max's tract of land. The flickering flames revealed the occasional pair of armed guards standing watch, and at least 3 large shipping containers outfitted in an "T" pattern that I would soon learn were the sleeping quarters and an office in one. A fourth shipping container off to the side looked to be used for storage. On the outskirts of the field, other camps were set up to accommodate the miners and those dwellings took the forms of tents, thatch huts, and the like. Dimly visible through the darkness was the outline of the large fuel tanker I had heard so much about, and the broken down crane. It was finally time to see what this place was all about.

"No place like home," Max quipped cheerfully, as he lithely sprung out of the confines of the Land Cruiser. "Let me show you where you'll be staying."

Tamba went right to work grabbing a ten-gallon gas container as he told Max he was going to refill the engine. Max thanked Tamba and asked him to meet us inside when the car was refueled.

The three containers were two bedrooms and the middle container was like an entrance and common area. The bedroom to the left was Max's room. Also there was a woman there when we arrived. I never went in that room but I glanced in as I passed it the first time, and I could see there was a bed. The container or bedroom to the right was where I would stay—it was just an army-style cot. The room was empty otherwise. As I put my bag down, lights came on and I could hear the generator hum. Max disappeared into his room. I figured I would go back outside as there was electric light now, and I could get a better look at the place. Right outside the repurposed shipping container that was Max's room, there was a pretty large screen tent with plastic chairs and a plastic table in the middle of the tent. There was an ashtray on the table. I sat down and lit a smoke.

I remember sitting there thinking, and not wanting to forget the moment. Here I was again, in literally the middle of nothing—just jungle and the occasional tribe. And this felt different, different because this was a leased place—this was, in the government's eyes, completely legal.

I was feeling a bit victorious. Just the fact that I was there and knowing that even if the rest of the world wanted to come, you couldn't get there. There were no hotels, no cars, no open services, and we were past the point where white men were even allowed. The way that I had gotten here was the only way one could get here, so I felt like I had somehow made it to Mars—but a Mars where treasure was not far from under foot.

I was taking everything in I could see from my vantage point, and even inside the screen tent I felt like someone was watching me—in Africa, some-one is always watching. Tamba had disappeared as well. I lit another cigarette. I could see not only the outline of the tool shed but a faint light from inside. There was a Yamaha 125 motorcycle sitting towards the front of the tools that were piled in the open entrance. The moonlight was bright at the moment, and I could see the way the pit had been graded down with the crane. The best way to describe it is if you took an ice cream scoop off the top layer of a fresh carton, just one scoop. But you could fit perhaps 20 cranes inside that hollowed out bowl of earth. As that gravel had been lifted off one layer at a time, it was transported a short distance to a gulley where you could see they had been washing the gravel. Max had a retention water tank to capture rainfall and the water pressure was provided by gravity.

Max never did come back out. Maybe he fell asleep. I put out my ciga-rette and went inside to sleep as well. I was happy to see we had running water and a toilet, in the morning. There was also a water filtration system with an ultraviolet light to kill bacteria in the water. I still planned to stick to my bottled water and trail mix for as long as possible. Max was already busy running around outside and ordering people around to finish one task or another, he saw me and gave me a hearty, 'top of the morning' in his best Irish accent. He approached me and said, "I have to run around to some other villages today. I've got business to take care of, and I'm looking for a part for a broken pump. While I'm gone, you are in charge. There isn't anything that needs doing but something may come up. I'll be back in a day or two."

Max continued to move around frantically checking on a sea of minutiae before his departure. "Tamba is coming with me as well. Follow me back inside for a moment," he said as he pivoted and started back towards the shipping containers. Back inside the sleeping quarters, Max emerged out of his bedroom with a gun holster. In it was a Russian-made Star 9mm semi automatic handgun. Max handed it to me, and said, "Being from Miami, I'm sure you know how to use this."

I didn't know how to use it, and I wondered what Max had heard about Miami.

"Do you think I'll need it?" I asked, and he gave a noncommittal shrug, saying, "It's not entirely out of the question. I don't think the rebels will be back here. We have a large armed population and at the moment there's nothing to take but if we make a diamond find..." Max clasped both hands together. "We lock down the village and no one is allowed in but people going out is the real concern. If word got out that we had hit a large vein of diamonds they would be back here with all the force they could muster. Anyone seen trying to leave during such a time will be shot by the guards on duty."

I took the gun and stashed it in my room. I didn't want to seem like I was being too cocky or boss man like to the villagers here; there were plenty of guns outside anyway. Besides truth be told, I don't think I could shoot a child, even if he was carrying a rifle.

Again I sensed that I was being watched. I also had that great feeling of 'here I was standing on this plot of land in West Africa, and technically "in charge",' whatever that meant. I took it as an honorary title. If you ever think you are really in charge, try telling someone else's dog what to do. I am not equating the villagers to dogs but the analogy still fits.

I began to look around the place. The space that was leased was a hectare and most of it was untouched. They had dug Marrakesh pits all around the property trying to determine where to begin to grade. That was one of the reasons why it was dangerous to walk around at night. These pits were deep, some were fifteen to eighteen feet deep, which was how far they had to dig down to hit the gravel. Once gravel is hit, samples are scooped up and checked for diamonds.

I wanted to have a look at these pits. There was an old villager whom Max had referred to as Pa. I asked Pa if he would accompany me on a walk about the property. Pa had no shirt on but he wore a brown wool beanie. It seemed like he never took it off. His face had these very deep and prominent ritual scars. As we walked along looking at the property, the surrounding jungle and the Marrakesh pits, I made the mistake of asking Pa about his facial scars. He stopped and turned suddenly, his entire body tensing as though he was preparing for violence. He locked eyes with me. I had stopped in my tracks. "I will forgive you because you are a foreigner," he finally decided after a moment of long, uncomfortable silence "But it is very insulting to ask a man about such things."

I apologized sincerely, aware that I had violated a taboo. His face visibly softened as did his tone of voice. "Let us continue with our mission. What would you like to see next?"

"Pa, I have never held gravel from a pit. Could you enter the pit and bring me up a handful of gravel?"

He agreed readily and we stopped at a pit we happened to be passing by at that moment.

"How about this one?" I suggested. Holes in the shape of rectangles are dug into the wall of the pit for foot and handholds. Pa was now using these as he descended. He was being very careful as sometimes scorpions and snakes fall into these pits. Once he reached the bottom, he grabbed a big handful of the gravel and then he ascended using only one hand and his two feet of course. He handed me the sample which he had brought up. I took it with both hands and thanked him as he emerged over the lip of the pit and we began walking along again. As we walked and talked, I was slowly disintegrating the gravel with my hands, feeling for any rocks that may be hidden inside. Like some kind of sorcery, when I got down to the very last bit of the gravel, I felt the shape of what I knew was about a one-and-a-half carat bolex stone pressing into my palm. My very first time near a Marrakesh pit, my very first time holding the gravel that contains diamond, and I had actually found one. It was unbelievable, I didn't show the stone to Pa, and I was sure he hadn't noticed. I had just been casually crushing the moist gravel between my fingers and letting it fall to the ground. I put the diamond in the pocket of my jeans. I finished my walk with Pa and was sure that I had kept a poker face, though a part of me wanted to jump up and down and scream that I had found a diamond the very first time I held gravel. But something told me that would not be smart. I was very excited and was proud of the sheer discipline I exerted to keep calm and quiet. This was exceptionally important because the Marrakesh pit the bolex stone had come out of was just *adjacent* to Max's tract of land. You had to cross Max's land to reach it but it wasn't his yet. We would have to lease it from the tribal elders that controlled it and then we would be free to claim the diamondiferous area we had just extracted a stone from.

After the walk, I went into the screen enclosure and I was having a water and a cigarette. I looked around very carefully and could see no one close enough to see me. I took the bolex stone out of my pocket and got a good look at it in the daylight. This stone was clean, small but super gem quality. I wanted to put my loupe on it but that would be too obvious should anyone be watching. With the naked eye in the bright light I could see no inclusions, this little stone would probably become a.75 carat round cut, and would fetch possibly $3k. I couldn't wait for Max to return, we had to dig in that hole. I went back inside my sleeping quarters and opened my duffle bag. I took a pack of cigarettes and I opened them in order to get the cellophane that they come wrapped in. I carefully put the stone into the cellophane and I wrapped it tight. I don't know who else does this but when I travel and I'm using a duffel bag I use one side of the bag as the dirty laundry side and the other side of the bag as the clean side, I placed the stone under the dirty side at the very bottom, and then I placed a case of bottled water on top of the laundry. This wasn't going anywhere, I told myself. I spent the rest of the day on a sort of adrenaline high, I couldn't believe my good fortune. I was standing in Africa for less than one day and as of this moment, I was the only one that seemed to know that one of those pits was good. I know no one else knew it because it was like Alusaine had once said, "If a single diamond is found in a man's yard, by the next day the whole house is gone." I spent a little time checking out the red Yamaha motorcycle, it was older but in great shape, the tires were low because it had been sitting since the rainy season, the key had been lost and could not be found so there it sat for months. It was a bit past nightfall now and I knew Max wouldn't be back. I grabbed some trail mix and a bottled water for dinner. I sat out in the screen tent smoking cigarettes until probably ten or eleven at night, then I washed up in the bathroom, running water especially filtered running water was a luxury up here. I felt really good about our prospects. Pun intended. I fell into a deep sleep.

I woke up the next morning about an hour and a half after sunrise. Max had returned to the mining site sometime between the time I went to sleep and now, and there was a big ruckus building up outside. I had absolutely zero idea about what was happening but Tamba was standing outside in front of the screen tent and he was gesticulating with his hands as he spoke to a group of men who were all yelling and gesturing back at him. I saw Max unloading something from the Land Cruiser and walk towards the shed with it, calmly as if nothing was going on. But the argument was getting ever louder and men were pouring out of the jungle from three sides, not just a few men but dozens. The men were all arguing in krio and I could understand very few words, sometimes they chanted the words "No more slaves", "No more masters" but Tamba would speak loudly for a moment, and even before he finished yelling, the men would truly erupt in a loud chorus of "no". This exchange took place a few times and on about the third or fourth time, Tamba, who towered above every man there, reached out and gave a man a very hard slap on the face with an open palm. I can only really call it what it was—a devastating bitch slap. The man crumpled to the ground like a bag of bricks dropped off a ladder. There was a stunned silence for a moment, and then one man with a heavy accent said words to the effect of, "When a black man slaps another black man in his own country, for the sake of the white man, who was told not to be here in the first place, it is an example of the evil the white man brings!"

The crowd had grown to a few hundred people and now they were chanting in unison "No more slaves, no more masters!" The men in front of Tamba continued arguing with him still mostly in krio, and there was some pushing and shoving taking place, and you would hear that chant break out in another part of the camp as word spread about what was happening. "No more slaves, no more masters!"

Max came walking past me and he said very conspiratorially "The old village farts stole that lease. Those are my Marrakesh pits." His eyes glanced in the general direction of where Pa and I had been yesterday. "Whatever you do, don't show any fear. If you do, you could be in big trouble. This is about you as much as it is about anything else." I was surprised but not afraid, I hadn't done anything that I could think of. And then it hit me—the bolex stone I found yesterday. I spoke up, "Max, I think I have an idea. Only one truly noteworthy thing happened yesterday. I have something to show you." We entered the makeshift dormitories I pivoted into my sleeping quarter and I opened my bag. I moved the water and put my hand under the laundry to feel for the bolex stone, but it was gone. I couldn't find the cellophane I had placed it in, I carefully but quickly took out the whole pile, then the other side, then everything in the duffle bag, everything was there even the pack of cigarettes with the missing cellophane, but no stone was there.

"Max, I think I've been robbed."

"What do you mean robbed?" Max asked, sounding a little confused.

I explained what had happened yesterday with Pa. "Holy shit." Max said as he peeked outside the door. "You can't stay in here. It will look like you are hiding. Go outside calmly. Keep some distance from the crowd but don't show any fear. I know exactly what this is about now," he said. Someone saw you make that find, and that should have been our lease option. I'm going back to speak with the elders," Max said and left.

I literally took a couple of deep breaths to steady myself. My hands were shaking a bit. This was exactly what Max had said they shouldn't see. To them, he later told me, showing fear or nervousness when you are being accused of something is like an admission of guilt, and right at that moment the very superstitious group was trying to decide if I was evil. A lot of things were still decided on the bush by consulting voodoo.

Apparently, yesterday I was being watched closely, probably by more than one of these men, and probably with the aid of binoculars. They had seen the find, and I can only guess that they must have some way to peek inside that container. The cellophane and the diamond were gone, someone had taken it and they knew that the Marrakesh pit was good and should be excavated. They obviously swiftly negotiated rights for it—as Max had just become aware of it—and now the pit was theirs—and from their perspective, I had stolen something from them yesterday.

The sight of me was just making matters worse, and I was getting the occasional jeer and things were being said to me that while I couldn't understand exactly what they were saying, I knew it was meant to be insulting. They certainly weren't flowery compliments on my hair, which was almost down to my waist by then. I walked over to the tool shed and for some reason I sat on the motorcycle. I heard a few people say, "It doesn't work", "There is no key for it"… things to that effect. And then I remembered an old trick. Don't ask me how I came across this trick, but older model Yamaha motorcycles had one very easy hack. Under the gas tank, there is a set of cables that go from the ignition to the battery and this cable has a small electronic box in the middle of it. That box is a plug and the design flaw was that if you pulled that plug apart it completed the circuit and had the same effect as turning on the key. As soon as I remembered this, my fear turned into a little hope. I was about to look like whatever the opposite of being afraid to get hacked to death looked like. I set the choke and gave it a kick, "That not gonna start man, there is no key, they done toll you datPadi", "Go on now leave it alone".

I kicked it again with a slight turn off the throttle and the 125cc, 2 stroke was alive. I glared at the men who stood in the direction of the voices, put it in gear and threw a bit of dirt as I headed for the generator, there I put petrol as they call it in the motorcycle from gas cans meant for the generator. Once filled, I noticed the yelling had subsided and all eyes were on me. I got back on the motorcycle and started riding around the rim of the large ice cream scoop in the gravel that I described. I had no helmet and my hair was in a ponytail just waving in the air behind me. I did a few of my best tricks, including a wheelie almost the whole length of the gravel pit and a series of donuts in the middle, I felt I was putting on a show for my life, truth be told. I saw Max pulling back into the property, and I began riding around the Land Cruiser and hooting like a cowboy at Max. I saw him smile and as I passed by the driver's side window, he said, "I think you are over compensating." Which made me genuinely begin to laugh. Which made me look all the crazier given the current atmosphere. I rode the bike wheeling on the rear tire back to the front of the tent. I stalled it purposely, put down the kickstand and got off the bike. "Here is your motorcycle back. You will never need a key again." So a few of the men came over and looking closely at the ignition they could see I had not harmed it in anyway. "Try it," I said to one of the men. He got on it while everyone was watching and he kicked it one time, it came right to life, he put it in gear and smiling wide, he rode it away, pretty soon they were taking turns riding the bike.

"Okay," Max addressed the mostly pacified crowd. "We have to stay calm and do everything by the law."

"I have been to the village elders and a few of you have taken the lease right from under my feet," he said, pausing to take a breath. "And I accept that. But we have an issue. You cannot get to that piece of land unless you cross through mine and I don't want the traffic right through the middle of my operation." Another pause as his eyes read the faces in the crowd. "But I am willing to make a deal."

"If you want easement, you must walk around the gravel pit where we are grading, I know it's twice as far but this is where we will be working too, and we have to try to get along. Now that you have seen that my guest has good magic, you must accept him as if he were me."

The men talked among themselves; some grumbled, but for the most part it was by all appearances a deal. I didn't see any formal handshaking going on—it's just not their way.

Tamba had his rifle back on and now he was walking along with a small group of the men he had been arguing with, among them the man whom he had slapped. The bush is strange in this way, I've seen a group of young men hanging out as friends, and culturally they are just more affectionate. They may walk along hand in hand for a moment or with an arm over a shoulder. But these are the same young men that can become 'short sleeve, long sleeve' kind of brutal. It was another one of those striking contrasts I kept seeing.

Since a diamond had been found, no one could leave until the excavation had been completed—this is to prevent a rush on the land. They weren't saying who found the diamond. In fact, they gave no details at all other than the lease was held by the village elders since they were first to hear of the find, and that the Marrakesh pit where I found the stone just so happened to be the epicenter of the dig. The former also meant that they would not be selling any diamonds to us; they would be obligated to offer them to their benefactors first. The so called benefactors of the elders were the current administration and the cabinet. They were the target of the RUF because they were supposed to provide infrastructure for this exchange with the village elders, but they weren't. They never kept their word to the people. This is the way business was done in the bush. And I would be very surprised if it still isn't that way today. It's like every couple of generations, there has to be a change in the guard, so to speak. It's the next generation's turn to get a piece of the pie. This is the government that the rebels were protesting against and beginning to maim and kill for. But I couldn't help but think even if the RUF started and ultimately won a civil war, in the end, they would just be installing their own puppet regime.

I do know this, I was very nervous about what I was hearing from the miners and villagers who liked talking to me. I gave a wide berth to anyone who looked upset by my presence. What I was hearing was a lot of growing support for the RUF, because they were promising a more equitable distribution of diamond wealth, and a lot of the miners like the ones working here resented that diamonds over 25 carats had to just be handed over to the government. And the government would be the ones setting their own price for what they would pay for the stones as well.

By sundown that day, and without any heavy machinery whatsoever, the area looked like the army corp of engineers had used tanks and earth-eating machines to uproot every tree, every bush. It defies description, and they had done it all by hand—just sheer numbers is what they had. As I photographed those men and what they had done, I thought what if they themselves became RUF.

Not every day was filled with excitement and riots of which you were the cause. The days that followed were hot and boring. We had been obliged to stay while they completed their dig. I wasn't very far from Alusaine by car but he didn't even know I was here. At least as far as I knew, he didn't know. It was frustrating to not be able to go check on the status of the village. I was wondering if they had been in conflict with rebels, how mining was going, how well they were supplied. Max kept assuring me that whatever problem they had been having with the RUF, it had been handled because if something major had happened over there, we would hear about it. And so far he was right, no news had traveled down the grapevine, which in all likelihood meant status quo.

On about the fourth day of their dig, there was suddenly a lot of excitement over in the mining areas. The men were hugging and smiling. They had graded down to what they refer to as a vein, and then they had continued to grade very slowly and carefully removing gravel layers with great care until they had completely uncovered this approximately 6 foot stretch that was about a foot wide at its widest point and a few inches at its narrowest point, and there were just diamond shards, like a 6-foot tall bottle had been laid down and crushed right there. It was one of the most amazing sights I have ever seen. This was the stuff of legend. I had to buy some of these diamonds.

They made a bit of a show. The village elders came to the mining site in a colorful procession of priests, princes, and other local dignitaries complete with umbrellas for shade and a woman fanning them all with large fans made out of banana tree leaves. Their wives were dressed very colorfully as well and wore intricate head ornaments. They walked from their SUVs that they had parked right where Max had asked them not to cross, a deliberate unhurried walk. They had to walk up a short but steep incline and then it was a straight path 100 yards or so—the same stroll I had taken with Pa. That's how close that find was to the land Max had. I was truly astonished. The elders and their much younger wives stood over the incredible find now as a photographer took pictures of them. One of them said something that made the others laugh and they seemed pleased and happy.

A watcher is always present when miners are mining, and they are incredibly good at their job, they can tell if a man has found a stone by the look on their face sometimes. They have become very proficient at spotting anyone trying to steal. Still occasionally someone got away with it. In this case, there was no need for the watchers and the elders plucked samples only to inspect them and show them to their wives and then casually toss them back in the pile. Meanwhile ten feet away was a guy who had no shoes and was dressed in donated clothes. There were stark contrasts all around. But tonight there would be rice and beans and bread in the village.

It seemed to always be a case of feast or famine. Those diamonds were quickly gathered up, and the boss, accompanied by a dozen armed men would transport those diamonds to Freetown that very day. They moved quickly to avoid being robbed by anyone. But the main worry these days was the RUF. Where they stored them or how they got them to Belgium for processing I don't know, but those diamonds would wind up on the open market as gems eventually.

So just like that, the lockdown ended and everyone was once again free to come and go. Finally, we could go see Alusaine. It was really bothering both Max and me that we were so close and yet so far from having the legal rights to that rich slew of beautiful, rough stones. And who could blame him? He had invested so much effort, so much time and hard work and just a football field away they had just recovered millions of dollars worth of rough like the mines of Cleopatra were underneath their feet waiting to be discovered. What made it a little more painful was that if I could have told Max about the find in private like I had intended to, that would have been our find.

I had one long shot in my mind and that was my trillion guy. How I hoped he was still carrying those beautiful trillions on his belt loop.

Max was an early riser and it was still dark when he woke me up to ready myself for the trip to Alusaine's village. We had coffee and I had a handful of trail mix for breakfast. At least the coffee was strong. Max always let the coffee water come to a rolling boil for about 5 minutes before we used it for coffee so it was safe to drink. This was on top of the filtration that came first.

We arrived in the village center about an hour after sunrise and there was a noticeable change in the atmosphere. The village had expanded and amongst the new construction were a few more wood homes that had been built near the town square as well as a general store with a new looking sign that read "General Store" in white paint. There were people beginning to move about and as we got out of the Land Cruiser I saw one of our generators being carried towards the bush and then I noticed a couple of my water pumps.

I tapped Max on the shoulder and pointed towards them, "There goes my generator and my pumps."

He looked interested as his gaze followed the men transporting the various mining implements. "How much equipment did you leave here"?

"Quite a bit" I answered, "enough to get them working. I left them a car as well but someone's since taken it." I realized I had not contemplated how Mohamed was doing since I had arrived. I hoped he found his way to safety.

Alusaine looked happy to see me—that was a good sign I thought. We greeted each other with a handshake and a little shoulder slapping. I started to introduce Max, who held up a halting hand and charismatically exclaimed "eh bo"

"I be knowin' him for a long time before you," Alusaine said as he cupped both hands over Max's in a vigorous handshake.

"Yeah, yeah that's right that's true," Max said.

"Ah forgive me for forgetting so now we are partners too" I said to Alusaine, gesturing towards Max.

"Okay very good Mr Mark. Before we speak of business, please allow me to show you the changes I have made since you were last here," Alusaine said, as he pointed out the new wood homes and the general store.

"Yes," I said. "I noticed the changes as soon as we arrived; I like the store."

"Yes, come let me show it to you," Alusaine said excitedly. We walked in to see a few isles of sparsely stocked shelves, a few soaps, a few canned goods including those tins of sardines. There were quite a few locally produced items. A soda brand that came in orange and grape flavours, a small glass box with rice balls, and some kind of breaded curried goat type of pie. All in all, it was a rather good start, I thought.

And I told him so. "I'm impressed, Alusaine,"

Max chimed in. "Yes, I am too. I didn't know this was here."

"It's only a short time here, maybe two months," said Alusaine. "Come, come let me show you around. There is more."

Next we entered one of the wood homes. The first thing I noticed was that it had an actual floor—a wood floor at that. "Mr. Mark, I never live like this before. Not until you came," he motioned us down a hallway. "Follow me into this room," he said, and we stepped into what must be the closest thing to a mancave in all of Sierra Leone. "You see this?" he asked, pointing at the bed. "This is a water bed—it is filled with water!" his voice rising with excitement. "And this look at my stereo system!" It was a rather large boom box with lights on the speakers that changed colors as the music played. "This is all thanks to you. You have changed my life". So, for a minute, I was happy Alusaine was happy, and at least Max was smiling. I wanted to let him enjoy his moment but I was dying to see one thing above all else. How had my play turned out? Would I be able to buy as well as last time?

"Okay my friend. I am happy too. Happy for you. But I am dying to see the parcel you have made for me to purchase," Alusaine nodded vigorously. "Yes, I have for you. I have a lot. Let me collect it. Make yourself at home until I return".

Max and I sat there conversing about the possibilities. Max wanted to return to his mine and begin digging and moving gravel by hand with shovels and washing as much as he could. He said he too could guarantee some samples. I was thinking that he had been somewhat impressed by what I had done with Alusaine and how Alusaine spoke of me. His interest in getting the heavy equipment here was rekindled, and I think his belief that I could do it was now reinforced. In for a penny, in for a pound, if we had left this much money here before what's to say we wouldn't do it again. We'd have a better guarantee with Max than we had gotten from Alusaine.

Finally Alusaine returned to us, carrying a coffee can that was about half-full of rough stones. He was excited to show me, and frankly even Max perked up. I peered expectantly into the can to see nothing but industrial quality diamonds. There were many yellow ones. I will admit and today the market has changed considerably. Once thought of as undesirable, yellow diamonds are now in fashion. I lowered the can to waist level and shook my head in disappointment.

"Alusaine, there is nothing of gem quality here. All of this is useless to me". We need exactly what we discussed and exactly what we bought last time," I said and stepped out onto the new wooden porch to get better light. I was able to find nothing that I thought I could use. Even the yellows were not completely formed and in most cases, they had inclusions you could see from a mile away. There was one very curious stone, it was small maybe 2 carats but it was black, not in the way a very large inclusion can appear black inside a diamond—I had seen plenty of those. This was apparently a black diamond by color. I can't say for certain because I didn't test it or even look at it with a loupe. I was deep in the disappointment of not seeing what I expected. I stepped off the porch getting a little angrier with each passing thought. We had talked and talked, how could he possibly even think this trash was acceptable. I turned holding the can up like I was about to make a toast, and I turned it upside down letting the entire contents spill onto the red soil.

"This wasn't our deal, Goddamn it, Alusaine!" Just then I saw another of the pieces we had purchased going by in the hands of people who were outsiders to the village, I couldn't even pin where they were from. That was the last straw for me. And I ground my boot heel into the pile of inferior stones I had just spilled.

"Industrial grade shit." The stones made a scraping sound as my heel twisted atop of them.

"Look at my gear all over the place!" I half shouted at him throwing my arms wide. My investments truly were scattered about doing anything but mining.

"You don't think it's easy to see what is going on here? How did you get half of a large coffee can filled with this shit?" I didn't wait for an answer, "I'll tell you how you did it—you used my equipment, my fuel, and you ate my rice while you mined. You've sold or traded the good stones and saved the crap no one wanted for me". Alusaine's face dipped in displeasure and what appeared to be a semblance of guilt. "There have been gun battles fought in my village." Alusaine fidgeted as he spoke. "And I had to make some deals. Mr. Mark I beg you please try to understand. Things changed and I had to change our deal, but we can make a new deal now". I was losing patience with the concepts that pacts were a malleable thing.

"Man, you're crazy, how am I supposed to trust you again?" I gestured towards the half empty fuel tanker a few dozen yards away that still bore the lumber yard's logo on the side.

"I paid ten thousand dollars for that fuel! Where is the other half?

"That's all that came," Alusaine replied flatly. I couldn't tell if he was lying but I suspected as much. "Great, that's just great... Okay, you want a new deal? This is our new deal: collect up all of my gear and the three of us will be back to pick it up the day after tomorrow."

"Mr. Mark, I cannot do that," Alusaine said.

"What? Why? Why can't you do that?"

"Because, I don't have it in my possession" I was becoming more dumb-founded by the minute. "I told you we had to make some deals" he said.

"Alusaine, that's theft. I have the bills of sale for everything here."

Alusaine's voice rose, "Mr. Mark, if you try to make them give it back, there will be big trouble!"

I shot back, "Alusaine, if you don't give it back, you are the one in big trouble! You have two days to get me a parcel that isn't a pound of shit or have my fucking gear ready for pick up".

"You cannot take that fuel," he insisted. "The village will stop running without it."

For the first time, Tamba spoke up, "Eh, bo. You see me. You know who I am. If the man has a receipt for the petrol, he gon' take his petrol, that is the law bo."

Max spoke for the first time, "It only seems fair."

Tamba added to that sentiment "The village gonna run the same way it always does when the fuel finish."

"How you gonna pull the petrol anyway?" asked Alusaine.

"How much fuel is left in it? Max asked. Tamba strode over to the trailer and started up the small ladder on the back of the fuel trailer, he deftly removed the cap, as if he'd done this before. There's a measuring stick that's carried on top of the trailer for this very purpose and Tamba was now pulling it out of the tanker and hoisting it up into the air. "There are about 1700 liters left!"

I gave Max a nudge on the elbow. "What's that in metric, Max?"

The miner scrunched his face up. "Let's see... It's about....450 gallons." "So including the trailer it's less than four thousand pounds" I said. After a little further calculating in his head, Max rejoined, "Hell yes. We can pull it." I turned to face the treacherous prince.

"Alusaine are you going to give me a hard time about this? We have to go mine on Max's property to make up for your end of our deal falling down." He didn't answer; he just turned on his heels and walked away. "We better hurry the hell up," Max said, fixing the chin strap of his hat back in place and giving a nod of approval.

"Yes, we had better." Max had a universal trailer hitch on the Land Cruiser, and it was a matter of removing a pin and flipping it, so the proper ball was facing up and backing it up to the trailer. Tamba was able to lift and roll the trailer the few inches it required to line up properly and he dropped the tongue of the trailer straight down on the ball and set the pin back in place, there were two chains to secure to the bumper of the truck and not a thought was given to any trailer lights. We took off just in time, as a small crowd had begun to gather and was taking an interest in us. We left them in a rising cloud of red dust.

"I think you would do well to just forget about your deal with Alusaine," Max said. "It's a problem businessmen have been freaking out over since they first began coming to Freetown." he continued. "You have a deal with someone, and suddenly their grandmother dies in the bush, and somehow that changes your deal."

Tamba spoke above the noise of the motor and the road. "Also remember what happened when you went out in the fields with Pa. You were very lucky that they returned to calm."

We drove the rest of the way back to Max's mining site pulling the fuel with just one incident, going over a series of deep holes with the trailer looked like it was going to be too much for the Toyota, but Max showed a little experience behind the wheel and got us through. I guess you don't survive up in the bush without learning a few things.

We got back late afternoon, the drive had taken twice as long as it would have without the trailer. But Max was upbeat to have fuel to work his own claim with. "First thing in the morning, we will start digging the gravel with shovels and we'll use the wheelbarrow to get the gravel to the wash rack," he said. "We are going to find some fine samples for you to take back." he smiled.

We sat inside the screen tent at the white plastic table in its center, the night was cool, there was a breeze blowing and I could smell the rain. I felt about as down as I had felt since I started all this. I was thinking this is as far as we are going to get. I didn't really have the resources to get that machinery over here. It would have taken some kind of miracle find and without anything substantial to create the kind of excitement required to get people to put in that kind of money sight unseen with the exception of the photographic evidence I could produce, it would not be easy. I explained all of this to Max and he listened.

"How many of your Miami friends have a lease like this one, in the middle of the richest soil on earth?"

"Max I've seen enough, if I could afford it I would have those machines here tomorrow, but I can't and people are skeptical. Anyway I'm not saying I won't try, all I'm saying is that if we had something to take back to Miami, I could guarantee the equipment."

We sat in silence for a while and as we did, we could hear two of the miners sitting over by the tool shed getting drunk on palm wine. We stopped talking just in time and the wind was blowing in the right direction, and we clearly heard one say to the other, "That Mr. Mark, he up to something."

"Yes mon," gossiped the other voice, "but maybe he brings luck."

Max slapped his hand down on the plastic table for effect, and he stood up and said, "Tomorrow we will find you the samples I promised, I am going to bed." And with that he just turned and left, but as he entered the sleeping quarters, he bellowed a thunderous "GOOD NIGHT ALL." I was surprised to hear half a dozen good nights shouted back from the bush in as many different directions.

"Good night Obito!"

"Good night boss!" and so on.

I smiled again too. We were still sitting here on top of a diamond mine. And I wasn't exactly broke as a result of all this.

It rained for a hard but brief spell after I went into the sleeping quarters. The water tank would be good and full but the gravel would be heavier. We had eight or nine miners, and Max and I pitched in while Tamba stood watch. We unearthed a handful of millies and a few yellows. I understood Max's belief that somewhere under this gravel there were diamonds, the signs were definitely here. We filled, pushed, dumped, washed, and repeated all day long. As you might expect, I developed a new respect for the men who worked like this every single day of their lives. And for them a large find didn't mean what it meant for me. Their lives are certainly made better by the finds that were made here but it hadn't been enough to lift them out of this standard of living, while for me these finds would provide oceanfront condos, new Corvettes, and lasting financial security, thanks to my professional broker. These folks didn't have a broker they could hop in their vette and go chat with. And this wasn't likely to change anytime soon.

Although they had not had heavy earth movers on the lease next door, they did have hundreds of miners who had a personal interest, as the find would belong entirely to the village elders and by extension each of them. There would be enough money for all of the men on that mine to take care of their families for a year.

"We're wasting time here," said Max the next morning before even saying hello or good day in his usually exuberant manner. "I have a better idea. Go and collect your things. We are going back to Freetown today."

We packed up a few things and within twenty minutes' time, we were set to head down the mountain. I said goodbye to the few men I had become friendly with, including Pa, and I wondered if I would ever see them again. This had been my longest stretch in the up-country. We had been here 17 days.

So the drive back to Freetown was uneventful. We rode mostly in silence. A strange mood was hovering over our little group and I felt we were all resisting a little despondency. It was just the result of being in the same company on this extended trip into the up-country, I told myself. But as we got closer to Freetown, we could see things were very different. The streets were totally deserted and UN trucks were patrolling the streets. Almost no civilian could be spotted on the streets of Freetown, and businesses all had their windows boarded up.

This was unsettling; a ghostly kind of feeling. It was early afternoon, as we got closer to Max's house, Max began to honk the horn to get the attention of the guards so they would open the gate, and as expected, it swung open as we pulled into the gravel drive. Max parked the Land Cruiser close to the house. We all went in to take showers. Max had a great set-up when it came to power and water. The generator house was well-built and set a few feet below the surface to contain the noise. And there was a big water tank attached to a great filtration system. Max didn't own the home, but he had a 40-year lease from the owners. Between what he had managed to get up-country and what he had here on the peninsula, you could say Max had accomplished a lot. It wasn't out of the question that we could find some-one who would lease the equipment for us just based on what I could show in photos and attest to having seen. Being back in the house with power and running water felt like coming home. I took a shower and changed, and Max had done the same. Tamba was downstairs in the guard's quarters.

We sat down. Me with a bottled water, and Max with a Scotch. I tried to seem upbeat and tell him that not all hope was lost. I had photos to prove everything and could make a compelling case.

"And if one guy won't do it, maybe the next guy will." I had said to him. "It's a mine in diamond country, a stunning sample fresh out of the ground would have been a great thing to have, but if we had already found millions of dollars worth of diamonds, we would lease our own machines and wouldn't need whomever it was we were pitching it to."

"You make a good point, Mr. Christian." Max fell silent and looked over his shoulders out the open French double doors admiring the ocean view. "Let's go to a little place I know of tonight," Max said, turning back. "It's a small place on the beach frequented by mostly locals, kind of a festive area. There is a jukebox and a little bar." The sun was cresting low on the horizon and already percussion rhythms could be heard emanating from deep within the jungle. "It's the native religion, quite common on this peninsula actually. Speaking of which, if you happen to meet someone with scars under their eyes, do not question them about them—they are ritual markings." I had already learned that lesson but I politely thanked Max for the belated advice.

When we left the house, we left on foot. "It's on the water's edge down this way," he said and pointed to a path in the rear garden that led into what looked like jungle to me, just dense with plants and palms, and trees. The footpath was well worn and it occurred to me that I never saw the guards or the kitchen help go out the front gate. As we walked the path, Max bent and picked up a few nuts that had fallen from a nearby tree. He produced a pocket knife and began to whittle away at the dark husk of the medium-sized nut.

"Do you know what these are?" he asked, raising an eyebrow. "No, I've never seen them. What are they?"

"I'm glad you asked," he smiled devilishly. "This is called bitta root. It's a true aphrodisiac. This nut is better than that little blue pill that just came out in the US for erections. Have you tried the blue pill?"

"No," I said, adding, "I thought your junk had to be broken before they prescribe it to you."

"Some wild musician you are," he joked.

"Common misconception," I responded.

"Well, let's put an end to that right now. Try this nut. Just chew it and swallow," he said, handing me a shelled nut. "It's just great for energy" he said. I hesitated. "Quit looking at me like I'm a perv you wanker," he said, and thrust the nut forward.

I took it and bit it in half and it was just like a bitter wall nut, very acidic. So I ate the other half. "Just one?" I asked grimacing as I chewed imagining these things making it to mass production packed into little medical wrappers stamped with a luridly grinning Mr. Peanut.

"One should do it," he said. "But put these in your pocket to take back to the States. You'll thank me."

The path continued for maybe half a mile before coming to an opening on the water, there was a small white sand beach with a couple of loungers on it. As we moved out into the open space, I could see a red neon sign inside a half open door of a small shack. As we approached, the door opened as someone exited the little bar and I could see the lights of a jukebox, which must have been changing discs as we arrived because almost as if on cue, it started to play *Beat It* by MJ. The little bar was kind of hopping, and there again was another stark contrast. The people in here all looked happy, content and smiling. Everyone was dressed well and in a party mood. I was the most underdressed for sure. But everyone was here acting like there weren't UN troops patrolling their streets and roving gangs of child soldiers chopping off people's arms at gunpoint. Max was receiving greetings left and right—the Africans all had a name for him. And I was hearing it even as he walked out of site swallowed up by the crowd.

Things were starting to feel like they were going by in a sort of dream state, where I'm moving in real time but everything appears to be happening in slow motion. There must be something to this nut, I thought to myself. As I walked further into the bar, I felt a little self-conscious for a minute, and to play it off, I began checking out the jukebox. I remember I was glad to see it was at least a modern jukebox as it played CDs. The selections were making me smile, not because I liked them so much but just because they were here, or maybe it was the bitta root. Colors seemed a little more vivid. In the jukebox was every MJ song ever recorded, including the J5. I saw by the counter on the digital display that there were songs on there for days. I saw a stool that was available at the bar, and having lost sight of Max I took the stool. I asked the bartender if he had an unopened coke in the bottle. Believe it or not, it's a distinction you need to make sure you make, when you are traveling there. They have a not-so-great habit of recapping previously opened sodas. He did and he opened it in front of me. I gave him ten US for the coke, and said, "No change, thank you." He nodded and rang a small bell on the register, inciting a chorus of "Eh bo!" from the crowd. It was then this beautiful smiling girl turned to look and we locked eyes for just a moment. It was one of those few times in life when your heart genuinely skips a beat, and for a moment you're the deer in the headlights. I smiled back at her because it was impossible not to. And I heard Max say, "Hey Mark, I'm stepping out for just a bit, wait here, run a tab if you like. I already told both the bartenders that you're my guest." And with that, he turned and left with a man who had been there when we arrived.

I turned to look for her again but she was out on the small vinyl square floor that served as a dance floor. She was dancing to Lenny Kravitz's *Are you gonna go my way?* I was thinking this place is surprisingly lit, and in an unlike me moment, I gave her a wink. It's not a big deal, I know, but it's just that I never do that. She winked back and it was on—she came dancing over and extended her hand. I also just don't ever really dance. It's not that I can't; I just always thought it was like a barely disguised pre-mating ritual. I've caught a lot of flak for saying that in the past but I still believe I'm right. And on this particular night, I danced my ass off. I felt as if I had energy for days and not a care in the world.

Her name was Charmaine, and she was pretty, yes, but she was clever and witty in a well-schooled, well-read sort of way. I guessed that she developed her sense of humor in England which is where she studied. But she wasn't from here, and she wasn't from there either. She was, she said, from Namibia, the Himba tribe. We had a lot in common. She had been raised in a London boarding school, I was raised in boarding schools in Florida. There are a few times in your life that you are face to face with someone that you consider yourself too lucky to have actually found. This was one of those times for me. We joked and laughed all night as if we were old friends. She drank water, as did I. We didn't want the night to end. And I asked her to come back to Max's house with me. We walked through the path in the woods like we were in some enchanted dream, and the moon and the stars were all the light we required.

I am not an author by trade. I didn't take journalism or even a creative writing course in high school. I have done exactly zero research for this book. I can only tell you this one story and I can only write this one book because I actually lived it. So I am not going to be very adept at writing the steamy sex chapters of an E.L. James' book. But suffice it to say that I had packed condoms in the duffle bag, and that I broke at least one—this bitta root was the real deal. As far as I know, you can still find it there easily.

So the sun was coming up when we fell asleep, and I slept the sleep of the dead. I woke up and it was noon, the sun was high in the sky and the room was getting hot, otherwise I might have slept the whole day. I sat up and Charmaine was gone. I could see into the bathroom and she wasn't there. I was disappointed she had left without saying goodbye, but as I got out of bed there was a photo of her on the dresser mirror. I picked it up smiling, and on the back was a Sierra Leone phone number. Yes! I thought. Life's looking up.

I put on my last fresh pair of jeans and I walked out of the room with no shirt. I wasn't expecting to see anyone as the house was very quiet, so as I rounded the corner, headed towards the kitchen to forage for coffee. I was surprised to see Max sitting at the table with two African guys I'd never seen before. They were definitely being conspiratorial and the moment they saw me, we all froze for a second. I turned to my right and pretended like I was going to the main bathroom all along, and I went in there and closed the door. What the hell was going on? And was that a diamond they were holding up? It was the size of a small boulder. I tried listening through the door to their conversation but they were very hushed and speaking in whispers. I did hear Max say, "And you can put a detector on it?" And just a few seconds after that the distinct beep of a diamond detector. I splashed water on my face and hair. I had brought nothing with me in the way of a toothbrush or a comb, and couldn't think of what to do except to just walk back out and head to my room to finish getting ready. They stopped speaking and there was an uncomfortable silence as I walked by. I went in my room and quickly stashed the photo of Charmaine. I finished brushing my teeth and brushing my hair and put on a fresh shirt, and just as I was walking out of the bedroom door, Max appeared in the doorway.

"I have your diamond to take back to your boss, Eli. I told you I would get it," he said triumphantly. "Feast your eyes on this," he said as he pulled his hand from his right pocket holding up a diamond the size of a golf ball. This was the big time. This would be my first contact with a monster stone.

"May I see it?"

"Quickly, the walls have ears and eyes" he whispered.

He handed me the stone and just as I held it up to the light, he snatched it right back, I had held it for ten seconds.

"We have to get out of here," he said. "I have your diamond as promised. But I have to accompany you to Amsterdam. Things are getting scarce here, and the truth is I'm flat broke. And I'll need a round trip ticket. I'll wait to hear from you in Amsterdam while you transport the diamond back to Miami and make your deals." he said.

"I'll be happy to do that Max, do you have a place to stay in Amsterdam?" I asked. "Yes, yes mate, I have a girlfriend there and I'll be fine once I get there."

"There's one thing I have to do. I have to let Eli know that we made it back from up-country and I have to advise him that I'm leaving back to Holland. We have to go into town and make a call," I said.

The problem was that there was no one at the telephone service station. And we couldn't get in touch with a soul. The American Embassy was destroyed already, so things were escalating with the RUF. I was more than just a little pissed off when Max went to the back of the Land Cruiser and lifted a cover in the rear of the cargo space that revealed a hidden smuggler's cubby. Out of it, he pulled a satellite telephone in a briefcase.

"What the fuck Max? You have a sat phone for 17 days in the fucking up-country and you couldn't let me call home?"

"Calm down," he waved his hand downwards. "This phone is on the chip of a textile mining company that's been here in Sierra Leone for a few years. I'm not technically supposed to even have it."

"What else are you lying about Max?" Things were becoming a little too cloak and dagger for my liking "Why won't you give me a good look at 'my stone'?"

"What's this then! One lie and suddenly everything is a lie?"

"I don't know, Max. You tell me,"

Max tersed his lips and spoke sharply, "Look, we have to get to the airport. I need to pack it up in something and we have to deliver it to someone there who can get it on board the plane for us. But we'll have to purchase tickets so I can give them a seat number. This is something I've done before and I can trust this person. By law this diamond belongs to the government, and there is a steep jail sentence for smuggling it out. That's the only reason I'm being so jumpy. We are not the only ones who know I have this diamond, and for every second we stand around holding on to it, we are in great danger—better believe that!" he exclaimed softly. Then lowering his voice, he added, "A lot of people here are beginning to think that the RUF are the Robin Hood of their era and they are passing information to them all the time. For a diamond like that, they would burn the entire city to the ground. Not to mention what they would do to us."

I called Eli on the sat phone and apprised him of everything as well as I could. He wasn't quite catching on to this fake boss thing, as he would ask things like, "Is this real now? Is this conversation real? Or is this practice? What do you want me to say?"

So I would just have a fake conversation with myself and pretend he gave me the answers I wanted. Just things like, thanks for checking in, I'll be expecting your call in 48 hours or I'll begin to worry. Things like that to make Max think someone knew or cared about where I was. For this entire trip, I had carried 4 bricks and spent very little of it. I peeled off five thousand for airline tickets standing right there at the tail gate of the Land Cruiser. "You aren't the only one with a little secret," I said, as I put the belt back on under my shirt. We had to take the ferry to Lungi to buy the tickets at the counter. Lungi and the ferry docks were the only place that looked like the Freetown I first saw—there were a lot of people trying to get out now. The schedules were all changed and these could possibly be the last flights out—and that was becoming a worry. Our flight wasn't until tomorrow; we still had one more night in Freetown.

We came back to the house. I guess Max was expecting to see Tamba and was now becoming concerned he hadn't seen him since the night we got back. I heard a sudden burst of gunfire, and some voices shouting, then we heard car engines. As they accelerated, the shooting noises continued as if maybe it were a running gun battle. The gates were locked and Max instructed one of the two guards still present to leave the generator off for the night.

I am not sure if Max stayed at home or if he went out that night, but the front gate was locked from the inside. I walked around outside the back yard close to the path, smoking a cigarette and thinking about Charmaine. Would she be at the little hangout tonight? I strained to hear any music but there was none to be heard. I started walking up the path. Last night it had seemed like an enchanted trail. I wondered, was it the bitta root? Was it the rumored bewitchments of this place? The path seemed eerie and somehow darker than last night. When I finally got to the other end, the little shack was boarded up tight and everything was still and quiet, maybe last night had been a last bash party. The trail seemed even more foreboding on the way back.

I wondered if Tamba had returned, I could use a friendly face.

The lights were off and it was completely dark as I walked back through the garden by the sunken generator shed and turned right into the courtyard, a shadow moved.

"Max?"

"No, it's Santa Claus," came the not quite British-accented wisecrack.

"Where have you been? Did you not hear the shooting?" Max was sounding kind of worried.

We spent the night sitting in the courtyard in the land cruiser.

"What are you going to do with this?" I asked, referring to the Toyota.

He shrugged, "I'll have to leave it at Lungi and hope that it's there when it's safe to return."

Finally, the sun was rising. The guards emerged from their downstairs quarters and asked if they should open the gate. "First take this," said Max, handing them a shoebox full of leones. "See if this money still has any value and spend it quickly on supplies and on generator fuel should any be made available. Try to spend it all today, and take good care of yourselves until I'm able to come back."

We headed out of the courtyard's gravel drive and onto the main road again. Our flight's departure time had been moved up by two hours, and I was glad we hadn't delayed getting to Lungi. Today was complete pandemonium. The ferry looked way overloaded and was listing badly to one side. This ferry, like the helicopters, that once flew here had sunk once. This boat was actually a replacement. It boggled the mind that they continued to overload it. Max had passed the diamond to his airport contact yesterday along with our seat numbers. The diamond should be tucked into the seat-back pocket of the seat in front of us when we board.

The ferry made it to Lungi and we got off with the herd. The airport was no less frantic. There were people trying to get out to any part of the world they could get to from here. The security was non-existent. We could have carried anything on board that we wanted to. The flight was completely full, and as promised, there was a small package in the seat-back pocket in front of Max. He gave a sigh of relief, but wanted to leave it where it was until after take-off. The KLM flight pushed off as soon as we had all sat down. As we were taxiing down the runway, a flight attendant crackled over the PA that if we were wearing glasses we should take them off and close our eyes as they were going to fumigate us and the plane. The air system sprayed out something that smelled like Lysol misting every passenger on board.

We were tired from the long night and even though this time the flight was packed, it still felt like home away from home. I slept for most of the 7-hour flight, and I assume Max did as well. The next thing I knew, we were touching down at Schipol airport near Amsterdam.

We are once again taxiing, this time towards our arrival. We hadn't declared anything on the forms we were given to complete, and after the cabin attendant had collected them, Max spoke, "You seem to have the proper temperament and composure to get this through customs. Would you mind carrying it?"

I just looked at him for a second, and reached into the seat-back pocket in front of him and took the small package it contained and slid it down into my boot. It just barely fit, and it was digging into my calf with every step. I hate last-minute felonies. I had to not let it draw attention to me passing through customs, which as you may know, is quite the long walk, and surveillance was everywhere. I got used to the way it felt by the time we exited the jetway and strolled pretty casually up to the first open agent. "Hello Sir, welcome to Holland. Do you have anything to declare?"

"No."

She examined my passport briefly and asked, "What was the nature of your business in Sierra Leone? It popped right back into my head from the first trip, and without missing a beat, I said, "Freelance photojournalist".

She shook her head side to side and frowned, "Terrible the atrocities that are being reported. Is that what you were photographing?" Her eyes caught the camera bag in my now open duffle. "I'm afraid it is, was, is, yes, I mean."

She laughed and closed the bag. "And what then is your business in Amsterdam?"

"It was the nearest place to Freetown where I could grab a decent shower." She just looked at me for a moment with a bit of a smile, and it struck me how pretty she was. I hadn't seen blue eyes in a few weeks.

"Also I have friends to visit on my way back to the States. I'll just be here a few days if all goes well".

She stamped my passport with a wink. "Enjoy your stay."

I sort of froze. Was it a Dutch thing to wink? Did she wink at everyone? Had she just read my mind?

I said, "You too," and immediately realized I was a dork as I fumbled and put my passport back into its place.

I met Max on the sidewalk. "I Love Amsterdam," said Max, taking a deep breath. "We should take the train to the city center and see about a hotel room for the night."

I agreed. We walked into the main building and followed the signs for the train. The train ride was relatively short, and when we arrived in the city center and walked out of the train station. It was like stepping back in time. The architecture is always breathtakingly beautiful and historic; centuries old in some cases. I was always struck by the idea that I was following in the footsteps of ancient persons atop stones that were set in place millennia ago. It was still daylight and we decided to just go with an affordable hotel. Somehow Best Western wound up fitting the bill and we took a cab to the one Hoofstrat. We got there just as it was getting dark. We checked in, I got a single room with two beds. We had a lot to discuss. The plane would not have been a good place for a discussion anyway, which is why we waited to even mention it.

The hotel was very old, how old exactly I don't know, but the way it was built seemed a little odd as it was very narrow—very narrow hallways, steep and narrow stairs, and of course, narrow rooms.

When you check into a hotel in Amsterdam, you have to give your passport to them and you get it back when you check out, of course. We walked into our room, and it was small but it would do. It had a light and a table close to the entrance and as you walked into the room it became a little wider and there were two single beds, one on each side of a tall open window. It was getting cold as Christmas time was approaching—we were already in December. I had a proper jacket in my duffle. Max closed the window. As I closed the front door, we threw everything down at the entrance and got down to business. I took my boots off and I opened my duffle, I found my loupe and my diamond tester and I took everything over to the little black table in the tiny entry hallway. Everything was almost comically too small. "It's time to take a look at this diamond," I said. I untied the twine that held the brown paper wrapped around the diamond. I switched on the desk lamp and sat down. This was a lot to take in, this stone, dependent on some known variables not working against it, such as faults, inclusions, cracks, could be worth a few million dollars. To be more precise, if it doesn't have any of those things I just mentioned, it would be worth that.

"Holy shit. Is this real?" I asked. It was like 30 carats, according to the gauge I was now holding it up against. I took the diamond tester from its case and turned the wheel that turns it on and warms it up, and I removed the black rubber tip protector that protects the element. I held the massive stone firmly in one hand and pressed the metal tip of the tester against the diamond, the red lights rose steadily to the top and the tester began to beep verifying the diamond. My heart was racing.

"Max, I am sorry I doubted you," I said, reaching for my loupe. I glanced at Max; he didn't look very enthused. In fact, he looked downright unhappy. I picked up the stone again and I began to inspect it through the loupe, "I think I see what you're worried about" I said. "The stone projects this rainbow from certain angles, and it's said that that can mean that there is too much tension in the stone, and therefore you assume a higher risk of it shattering into many smaller, and therefore less valuable pieces."

"Your man Ygal did a good job of teaching you," Max said.

"Max, this is no big deal. It's not even a problem," I said. "It more than achieves its purpose. You had me worried. Start picking out what options you want on those John Deere dirt excavators and movers; we're in business."

I placed the stone and detector down gently. "I'm going to take a shower and after you do, we'll go get dinner and a couple of celebratory Scotch whiskeys for you. Come on, Max cheer up, proof of concept is all we needed; you did it."

"Yeah, you're right," he said. "Okay alright then. Maybe you're right," he repeated. "Go on then. Start getting ready." He smiled, but it didn't look sincere. It wasn't until we went to dinner some place close to the hotel and Max had consumed a few Scotches that the truth began to emerge.

"Ygal did show you a lot it seems, but there is always something you haven't seen," Max began. "I myself was fooled."

I interrupted him, "Fooled by what exactly? The diamond?" He nodded yes.

I suspected something all along but to hear it confirmed was a very deflating experience, especially after having just told myself that whatever was eating Max, at least it wasn't the diamond. But he had lied and he had waited until I spent another seven grand to come back here before telling me. I had been trying to scam him in order to get me back to Alusaine, and it was a half-lie that I could easily get the machines Max had wanted. My entire goal for this trip was, in fact, to bring home as much rough as I could get my hands on. So we had both been lying a little, or maybe even a lot.

I needed an upper hand. This was clearly turning into a big game of cat and mouse. What then had his intentions been when we went through the trouble of smuggling out a fake stone.

"You heard me lying to Eli on the sat phone. This isn't going to sit well and it's going to be on you Max, you knew all along." Max had a fourth Scotch.

"Mark, just hear me out, please. You can take this stone back with you; it fooled both of us. It would be easy to see how anyone in the field would be fooled."

"I'm not going to get into this game of deception. You would have done better to just continue fooling me and letting me leave with the stone."

I held up one hand to pause his next thought, as it was occurring to me that out in the field, I would have been very, very leary of the first thing I noticed about the stone, and that's the rainbow that it's so clearly producing, and I began to voice as much to Max.

"I would not have purchased that stone, not anywhere near the price it would otherwise fetch, and by not nearly, I mean a small fraction is all I would have offered—" Max stopped me with a hand up in the air.

"BUT," he said, "some people *would* purchase it. The men that brought this stone to me have trapped many a novice buyer with this bait." Max was clearly feeling the whiskey.

"I'm going back to the hotel. I have to call Eli and tell him the truth as soon as I know it 'cause that's how we keep each other's trust, Max." He looked sheepish for a moment. I got up and left.

I was already in the room and on the telephone when Max gave a light knock at the door and came in. He went over to one of the beds and sat down. The phone was ringing in Miami as he did. "Hello" answered Eli. I was holding the handset but the ear piece was loud as hell. "Eli, it's me,"

He answered, "Hey, what happened? Did you buy the tickets to Amsterdam?"

"Yes, but I have some bad news. The stone we smuggled out isn't real diamond. Let's just say that Max here was less than truthful," I said. I was expecting Eli to play along, as if Max were in the room. But as I said before, Eli just wasn't good at taking the cue.

"Oh shit, did he find out we were trying to scam him?" Eli blathered on. "I knew that shit wasn't going to fly when you left. I told you it was a dumb idea; shit lease fucking machines all the way to Africa, I can't get a used car on credit."

I interrupted him by saying his name, "ELI"

There was a long pause. Max was looking me right in the eyes, and I was looking at him waiting for a reaction.

"Oh shit, can he hear me?" Eli asked.

"I can hear him," said Max.

"Let me call you back," I said and hung up. Now I don't know what Max heard. But I remembered an old saying that says in part, 'he who speaks first loses'. And I just stood there feeling pretty embarrassed. Max spoke first, "You are so honest. That's rare. I'm sorry for embarrassing you with your boss Eli, I am going to make this up to you I swear." What had he heard? He had seemingly totally misinterpreted the content of that conversation. Was it Eli's East Coast accent and unfamiliar American slang that made Max hear something different? I'll never know but he was clearly repentant for having lied to me and instead of being caught red-handed lying myself, I was seemingly suddenly absolved in Max's eyes. I remembered another saying, this one I knew who to credit for as well—it was Napoleon's words that came to mind. 'When your adversary is making a mistake, do not interrupt him.' I wasn't about to correct his assumptions.

"Okay" I replied cautiously "How are you going to do that?"

"I don't know at the moment but I'll think of something".

"Yeah, let's get some sleep then," I said.

I stripped down to my boxers and a T-shirt to get into the opposite bed. I was just drifting off to sleep wondering what his next move might be, when that question was answered. He was snoring like a stump grinder. All night long. I didn't sleep for shit.

Fortunately, Max was up soon after sun up. He had slept in his clothes. He took a loud piss in the bathroom and I thought first the fucking snoring.... He washed his face in the sink and used one of the guest towels.

"I will work something out. I have an idea for the stone. I'll be back I promise" And with that, he left with the fake stone. Somewhere along the conversation last night when he was explaining to me what the stone really was, he told me that the Africans call this mountain crystal. Today I think it was what is known as moissanite, a substance that appears very much like diamond and is second in hardness only to the diamond. It actually would have been a valuable find but not as valuable as if it were diamond. Today's diamond detectors have a setting to detect moissanite.

I waited until the next morning and I thought possibly this was game over. I was just about to book the next flight back home when there was a knock at the door. It was Max. He looked fresh and sober. He flashed a smile that could start a bushfire. "I have an idea to sell the diamond."

In many parts of Europe, you find exchange houses where you can exchange your currency for whatever the local currency is. They are normally very secure, and bulletproof plexiglass separates the tellers from the customers. The monies are kept in bank vaults and virtually every door is monitored and requires that someone buzz you in.

Max happened to know a money exchanger in Amsterdam. He was a reputed diamond buyer. Max knew him personally and said he knew "fuck all" about diamonds. He owned a 5-story building in the city; the ground floor was an exchange house and the remaining 4 floors were used as his home where he lived with his family.

He was Arabic and was otherwise a good businessman and a sharp individual. But he thought too highly of himself and that was his Achilles' heel. He was, "and this is very important," Max said, "very greedy. He would be a perfect target to pawn this stone off on."

"Great!" I said. "Why don't you just do that?"

"I can't take it to him; he would suspect something right away. But _you_ could. I know personal things that I can pass on to you; if you say certain things to him, he will believe you." Max insisted.

"What sort of things?" I asked.

"For starters," Max said, "he's been to the up-country. He's purchased diamonds in the village of Kamak, from the village elder himself. He considers the chief his friend; the chief's name is PaKamara."

"That's very good info indeed." I reached for a cigarette ignoring the 'no smoking' sign conspicuously posted by the door. "I could tell him that PaKamara entrusted me to bring him this diamond and offer it for sale exclusively to him."

"YES!" Max exclaimed. "That would absolutely explode his large ego."

"What's his name anyway?"

"His name is Fareed but he likes to be called Nick." Max said, "It's another one of those ego things; he thinks it sounds cool. You would be wise to use both names furthering your way into his trust."

I sat looking out of my hotel window at the limited view of the city street below. It was a beautiful day and the wind blew the white chiffon curtain into the room, bellowed it up and floated it momentarily before it lazily drifted back down when the wind subsided. It was reminiscent of something that I couldn't put my finger on; like *déjà vu* but in a comforting way. Max was still seated across from me on the bed he had slept on.

"Would it make sense to send me with the stone unaccompanied by anyone? I mean, would Kamara trust an American with such a valuable diamond?"

Max thought about that for a moment and his eyes lit up. "There is a place in the city where Sierra Leoneans hang out." He rose from the bed and grabbed his hat. "Come on let's go see who we can meet." I understood what he intended to do and I thought it was a great idea.

We had to do a bit of searching and that took us on a little tour of Amsterdam. We came to a large fountain in front of the Waldorf Astoria. There were a few people hanging around and a few young men who looked like they could possibly be from Sierra Leone. We approached a small group and Max said hello in Krio and a few of the men responded. I saw a guy smartly dressed in a light brown suit with a button-down shirt and brown shoes. I pointed to him and asked "Freetown?" He nodded one time yes and smiled. "Could I take a minute of your time, I want to ask you a question or two." I said.

"Sure; that's okay."

I held out my hand and said, "Pleased to meet you; my name is Mark". He shook my hand firmly and said "My name is Samuel but you may call me Sammy as my friends do." I said, "Let me introduce you to my partner; this is Max." "Pleased to meet you as well." Sammy said to Max extending his hand.

"Sammy, we were told by someone from Freetown that men looking for work can sometimes be found here, and I am wondering if you are one of those men."

"Yes that is precisely why I am here." Sammy said.

"We would like to offer you an opportunity that you look like you would be well suited for." Max said. "Sound interesting?"

"Of course" he responded. "Meet us at the Best Western on Hoofstraat as soon as you can; the sooner the better." I said.

He responded saying, "I can come with you right now."

"Perfect."

Back at the hotel, Max and I explained to Sammy what we were planning to do and what we needed him to do. His part was to be simple. He would come with me to the exchange house. We would tell the attendant or teller at the window that we needed to see Nick and that we had come from Sierra Leone, He would understand why we weren't able to call or telegram beforehand, and we could use the deteriorating conditions in Sierra Leone as an excuse. All Sammy needed to do at that point is to tell Nick that we had been sent there by PaKamara to see him with this diamond. He would say he is one of PaKamara's sons. After that I would do the rest. But he had to be convincing and be careful of questions that may come out of nowhere.

Sammy had this interesting little practice. He would do a ritual of sorts using paper and pencil. He would draw these series of symbols and made a series of calculations, which he said alerted him as to whether a situation would be favorable or unfavorable. He did the first of these small rituals as soon as I had finished telling him the plan. When he finished, and it took a few minutes by the way, he looked up and said, "This will work out good for us."

"I should say it will," I started. "For this introduction, we will pay you five thousand gilders—if we are successful."

He smiled, "It's working already."

We agreed that Sammy would return to the hotel tomorrow morning and we would attempt this then. We also agreed that Max would stay away and out of sight. I would meet Max at the Best Western when the deal was made. He took the stone, which was then in the right kind of paper, out of his pocket and put it in my hand. Everyone left and once again, there I was with my thoughts. I had the whole night to kill. I spent it wandering around the city (or 'wondering around the city'.). I went to the Bulldog at Leidseplein Square; I watched the street performers and wondered what their lives might be like when they weren't doing this. The nights were dropping down to the low 40s but that's not considered cold in Holland.

I was sitting in the Bulldog just having espresso coffee, but there were a lot of people sitting around me smoking some of Amsterdam's finest. More than once kind strangers offered me a hit by holding whatever they were smoking out to me and I could fully smell it, so the next thing I knew I was conversing with total strangers about what I had no idea. But suddenly, I decided that I should walk over to the McDonald's and bring chips for everyone. Chips are French fries in Amsterdam and they don't come with ketchup but rather with mayonnaise mustard mix. It sounded like a good idea at the time. But I was about to have one of the most embarrassing moments of my life thus far.

As I got a couple of blocks away from the Bulldog headed towards the McDonald's, I saw the band Cheap Trick. They were walking straight towards me on the sidewalk. Immediately, without really thinking, I exclaimed, "Hey, Cheap Trick!" Rick Nielsen said a really friendly and jovial, "Yes, that's us. How are you, sir?" and I responded with something like, "I heard your son's are doing great!" Rick shot at me a strange look. "Who?"

"The twins, of course, with their song *I can't live without your love and devotion*, The Nielsen Twins."

Turned out it was the 'Nelson' twins and their famous guitar player dad was Rick Nelson. Not Rick Nielsen. I realized what a stoner mistake I had just made, and slipped into the shadows of the street. Rick Nielsen, if you ever read this book, that was me in Amsterdam and sorry about that.

"I am stoned," I said to myself. "I'm not getting chips; I'm getting back to the hotel and in bed. I've got a crazy day tomorrow to say the least."

That was another night I slept well. The morning came and it was show time. Sammy was wearing the same suit. He still looked sharp enough and it just somehow looked the part. It was definitely the suit of someone who only has one and only wears it to job interviews or to court.

He came in and we went over the plan and who he was and tried to cover every conceivable question someone might ask. We felt very sure we had everything covered.

Sammy did his ritual with the paper and pencil, and again he lit up when he said, "This is going to be just fine."

We caught a cab to the exchange house. It was a busy city block. Directly in front of the exchange house was a large plaza and there was a cab stand less than a block away from the bank's front door. One city block over was a series of bars and establishments, I had our cab drop us off in front of a small Cafe that had a view to the building near the restaurant area. The open sign came on and without another word, Sammy and I crossed the street and headed into the bank lobby.

The lobby was large and had a long bench against one wall. As you walked in, if you walked straight ahead, you would walk right into the tellers' cage, which stretched all the way to the left wall. If you turned right upon walking in, you would be at the bench. The tellers were behind the plexiglass and inside the cage was a door into the main house. Also, there was a door into the main house on the same wall but out of the cage. So two doors, one in the cage one out; both went upstairs into the main house.

Sammy and I entered through the double glass doors and walked straight to the teller. There was a young man of about 25 behind the glass; he held a button to speak into a microphone.

"How may I help you?" His accent was Arabic.

"We have come a very long way to see Mr. Fareed, we have travelled from Sierra Leone." I said, "I am sorry for the short notice but we had no way to contact him other than showing up."

We explained that we were sent by PaKamara and that's all Mr Fareed would have to hear to want to speak with us. The young man obliged and entered the house through the door inside the cage. We waited for maybe five minutes and we heard footsteps coming downstairs behind the door in front of us, a second individual appeared inside the cage and pushed a button that buzzed the door in front of us open; there appeared the first young man.

"Okay, he's going to see you. Follow me." And just like that we were in.

The young guy led us up a flight of stairs and into an office where we were asked to take a seat. Within a few minutes he was with us.

"Mr. Fareed?" I asked, as he walked in.

"Ahhh hello Mr. Nick; it's so nice to see you again." said Sammy; He was a natural. "You're not going to tell me you don't remember me? I am Samuel the 5th son of PaKamara's. I was a little boy when you came to my village"

Nick was floored. "Yes of course, of course, I remember you; you have turned into a man!" Nick lied. "So how is your father Samuel?" Nick asked.

"Please, call me Sammy as my friends do. Father is well, but things are not well" Sammy said seriously. "And that is why my father has sent Mr. Mark and me to see you."

"My father has entrusted Mr. Mark with something that he wishes to show you." Sammy looked towards me, maintaining a saturnine mask.

"I've brought something to show you—that's true." I started slowly, "But we are only to show this to you. For obvious reasons, we don't want anyone else in this city to know that we have this. It's a 'for your eyes only' type of a deal. Can we please agree on this term of confidentiality before we proceed?"

Nick didn't hesitate a moment. "Yes of course, of course, I completely understand." I took the blue paper with the wax paper inside, out of the inside breast pocket of my leather jacket. Just the site of the blue paper made him catch his breath and let out a long "No. Is that what I think it is?"

I unwrapped the paper and Nick said something in Arabic and he got up and moved swiftly to the door to close it. He walked back around his desk exclaiming, "Ya Allah! Let me see that!" He held the giant stone between his thumb and forefinger and held it up to the unobstructed light of the glass window, the natural light that filled the room made the stone look even more impressive, but there was that glaring rainbow. Nick never mentioned the rainbow arc of light dancing across the stone as it caught the light. Instead he opened a drawer behind him and from it took a black binder and a loupe. He looked closely at the stone with his loupe now, and didn't say anything for several moments. He produced a diamond tester from that same drawer and turned it on. While he waited for the diamond detector to warm up, he looked up at me and our eyes locked. His face had changed. He seemed either angry or bewildered, I honestly couldn't tell. I thought, "Oh fuck; this might be going sideways here."

He pushed the tip of the sensor against the stone and up it went indicating diamond just as it had for me. He looked up again and said, "Just as I thought; it's fucking real" he said.

My heart beat steadied but his face remained fixed in that same charged expression. That wasn't anger or confusion in his eyes; that was greed—pure greed.

He put the stone and the tester down and opened the binder. "Come look at this. I want you to know who I am." He began detailing the entries in what was a scrap book of previous diamond buys regaling me with stories of guile and profit. There was even an outline of each piece of rough on each page along with the color clarity, carats and the most interesting to me, what he paid for them. I was playing along anyway but once I noticed that the prices were written in each one I began to get an idea of what number he might expect to hear. He truly enjoyed talking about each purchase and its value and its final sale price once cut and polished and in some cases even who bought them. They were all beautiful diamonds to be sure—there was no denying this gentleman was a serious diamond investor. But I think some early successes in the business had made him reckless. He was no longer even studying the new diamond in his presence but going over other old victories in his book.

We had been prepared to answer an onslaught of questions but he didn't seem to have any. I kept waiting for the obvious questions. Like why would I not have bought it first for which, I had an answer. But he never asked. I was back in my chair and Sammy was sitting calmly in his and we both listened to Nick go on about his purchases for a full fifteen minutes. He finally turned his attention back to the stone on his desk. "So PaKamara sent you to see me specifically? He was louping the stone again, and I could see he had a slight smile on his face. He placed the stone down on the paper. "I am glad you came to me and I am impressed by your find. I'm interested in buying. But I must consult with my diamond partner and let him see the stone." The more opportunities he had to discover that this stone was no diamond the worse so I tried to dissuade him "But PaKamara said you were the final decision maker, he was very clear that only you should know we have this stone in this city." Sammy adopted his solemn tone again and pronounced, "It is true, my father consulted the numbers in our presence and said to trust only your decision." Fareed looked a bit annoyed until he glanced at the stone again. He must have been very aware of how many tribes in West Africa rely heavily on their beliefs and since he had met PaKamara, he would know that he was pious.

"Then that only leaves price to discuss," Nick said finally. From a shelf behind his desk, Nick pulled down a special scale for weighing diamonds, it has a glass enclosure so that no outside force can influence the weight. He switched it on and opened the glass lid placing the stone inside. 31.2 carats.

"Very nice indeed," Nick said, more like he was talking to himself than to us.

"Our asking price with all due respect Mr. Fareed, will be the equivalent of 2 million USD." I said.

"I could give you one million guilder right now and it's finished. And I told you, call me Nick."

"That just won't do. I still have an obligation to Sammy's father. PaKamara and myself have already come to a personal agreement. Two million is our best price."

"Why are you not purchasing the diamond yourself?" Nick finally asked one of the questions I had been expecting. I saw this as my chance to make it about his expertise and to challenge his notion that he was such an astute diamond buyer.

"I'll be honest with you. I went to Africa for a different type of investment, I left machines and tools and transport vehicles there last year. I have been in the up-country for nearly a month. I left ten thousand dollars worth of fuel, and the emerging civil war has completely upended my deal. I have 40 grand in a money belt that has been digging into my back for a month and that's all the money I have left in the world, that and half the value of this stone."

I had his attention and he was listening. "That diamond could be worth upwards of 4 million dollars, once it's cut and polished. It's flawless and as white as a sheet of paper." I took the stone and let it catch the light producing the prismatic effect and then looked towards Nick to make sure it had his attention. I gestured towards the spectrum shining out of a bright white facet of crystal. "That rainbow hue is indicative of high tension in the diamond and whoever purchases it will be risking that it shatters into a thousand pieces when they try to cleave it. That's the only reason I'm not betting on a stone like this myself." For better or for worse, I had just put all the cards on the table. I needed to give him an opportunity to be contrarian to demonstrate that he was more knowledgeable about diamonds than I was, and to make it logically congruent for him internally to see why I would part with this stone instead of having it cut and doubling its value.

"I have a business partner who brings me stones from Sierra Leone. From Kamakwie." Nick said.

"Is he there now"? I asked. "No in fact he's just come back for the second time in as many months, and we are finding no diamonds. His big digging machine is broken and requires a part he can find only in America."

"What village did you strike a deal with Mr. Mark? I mean prior to PaKamara."

"I was in Kamalu." Nicks face lit up "Ah, we're practically neighbors! I run a mine in Kamakwie! My partner usually handles the management of day to day affairs." There was only one mine the Kamakwie village controlled—Max's.

"Your partner runs the mine and you manage affairs and accounts back here in Europe?"

"Well, yes, but I'm closer to the president than just a partner really. I control fifty *two* percent of the ownership of that mine after all."

"Why the emphasis on the 2 percent"? I asked

"Controlling interest." Nick smiled. "That way my partner cannot make any decisions without my approval."

"I can see exactly how all this could have come to pass. Kamalu is close to my place and even closer to PaKamara." I am satisfied that you and Sammy are telling me the truth." But I don't agree with you as far as the stone being a risk. All of my large stones have exemplified this trait." he insisted.

"You have purchased bigger diamonds than I've been able to, I will defer to your superior knowledge, however, I took a course in gemology, not an official one but I studied for an entire year. And to be fair it's one of the things I learned, I've never actually seen it happen myself so there is a possibility that I'm wrong."

"Yes, you see!" Nick exclaimed. "One whole year to an American and they think they are experts." Nick said looking at Sammy who was smiling now and nodding with Nick, "I have been going to find diamonds since Sammy here was knee high to a grasshopper. I will teach you Mr Mark!" Nick said. "But first we must agree on a price for this diamond."

"I've given you my level best price, Mr. Nick"

"Okay Mark, you are right about one thing, I do assume the risk for the stone." Nick said, changing his tone to boardroom cold. "You will accept 1.2 million in guilder and we will finish this now." Sammy's face was a blank canvas. It was all I could do to not accept the offer, but it was too low. If the diamond had been real, that would have been a red flag. No one gives away 3 million dollars.

"Mr. Nick, I will come down in price by 100 thousand dollars US. That's if you can do it right now. I will accept 1.9 million at the current exchange rate."

He leaned back and appeared to be deep in thought. We stayed silent for several minutes and I remembered a similar stand-off from my first trip. I thought 'I could do this easy—you're not even pointing rifles at me'.

"I can't do it today. I have to order more cash or the bank will not have funds for exchanges. If you are not taking it to anyone else, why don't you come back here tomorrow at ten in the morning? We are close on the price I think. And I can order more cash after you leave." Nick said.

"Why don't you leave the stone here for safekeeping? I have a bank vault after all." Nick said, as I wrapped the stone back up in the blue paper.

"No, that won't be necessary. No offense but the hotel has a safe as well."

"Okay, that's fine" he held both palms open towards Sammy and me. "I am only trying to help." Of course, that was true in a way. He was certainly trying to help himself. I could tell that this man's mind was caught in a tug of war between his greed and suspicion. He wants time alone with this stone to scoop out the fly in the ointment. This man may have been both vain and filled with avarice but there is nothing a proud man detests more than being outsmarted and Fareed's business acumen was insisting somewhere inside his soul that though this deal seemed sweet, honey is never far from the sting. I was working to give the voice of his greed more clout than his fear.

Sammy and I were escorted out of the office by Nick. This floor appeared to be for offices and as we went back out into the stairwell, I could hear a woman conversing with children in Arabic. The upper three floors were the home space, I deduced. We went down and it became obvious as we got to the door that someone was watching on camera and they buzzed it open for Nick right as we reached it. He held the door with one hand and we shook hands again and said till tomorrow.

Sammy and I spoke only briefly, I told him he had been fabulous, he was very satisfied and didn't seem to want any more money now that he knew how much I was asking, I had fully expected it to be the first thing he said. Instead he did his numbers ritual again and again he said the omens bode well for tomorrow.

"I am going to part company with you here, Mr. Mark. But I'll be back at your hotel in the morning." said Sammy.

We said good night and I caught a cab back to the hotel. There was a lot to think about, Max hadn't told me that he had a partner much less one that had a controlling interest in his diamond mine. That's two lies from Max in three days. And they weren't lies of omission—they were big lies. First, he had planned to send me home with a fake diamond and only alcohol had pried that loose, and I don't think he even considered that I might learn that Fareed was the actual owner of the mine.

I was sitting on the bed, and watching MTV Europe when on came the FarrCry music video *Loving You*. There was a beautiful model in the video who played my love interest. She was one of the few black Playboy centerfolds, a Miss November, her name was Stephanie Adams. There we were on MTV Europe. I forgot about the diamond business and became a band guy again for a little while. I was on the phone waking people up including Stephanie. She was thrilled to hear it playing on TV over the telephone.

We talked for half an hour and I went to sleep that night in a really great mood. It had been a super memorable night in Amsterdam in my hotel alone. Life is funny that way.

I woke up thinking today could be the day everything would change. 2 million dollars would go a long way with me.

And I had decided that Max had tried to play me once too often and that he was currently playing his own partner. That was all the justification I needed.

It was another beautiful but colder Amsterdam day. The sky was blue and clear and the air was crisp. We arrived at the exchange house about 10 minutes early, the bank was closed but the lobby doors were open so we went in and sat on the bench against the far wall to wait.

Sammy busied himself with his ritual again and again and I asked him to inform me what it had predicted or foretold, he shook his head yes.

The door of the lobby opened and in walked Nick, he was accompanied by two very tall Dutch-looking gentlemen, both of them wore impeccable black suits, white shirts and shiny black polished leather shoes. In fact, the only difference between their manner of dress was their tie color, one black tie with a white shirt, the other a dark blue with a white shirt. They had close cropped rusty blonde hair and looked like CIA agents, although I don't think they were. I don't know who they were but Nick, acting very rudely in my opinion, didn't even greet me or acknowledge Sammy at all. Instead he walked up, a coffee in one hand and keys in the other and he said, "Show these gentlemen what you showed me yesterday."

I took two steps forward and I looked at him very closely in the eyes, I looked up at the two yetis and I calmly said, "I don't have any idea what he's talking about."

And I just looked at him again. There was a stunned look on his face, but one of the two men said, "That's okay, I understand, Maybe some other time." and they excused themselves and left. Nick had turned to watch them leave and snapped his head back in my direction.

"Why you make me small boy in front of those men!" I think I had just had enough or maybe it was the arrogant demeanor he had just displayed but I turned and faced him

"You motherfucker—what's the very first thing I told you? What's the last thing I told you? What is the only fucking thing I told you!?"

"Forget it. At your very first opportunity, you broke the deal. I can find unprofessionalism like that in Africa. I didn't need to come all the way here to find it. It's your loss, Nick, you explain to PaKamara that you don't know how to even keep your fucking word. Come on, Sammy, let's get the fuck out of this waste of time."

And then I walked out. I was headed to the cab stand when Sammy ran up beside me.

"He wants you to come back," Sammy said, a little winded.

"I know. Come on let's go back to the hotel and wait for him to call." I said.

"Are you sure? I think he's sorry he made you mad," Sammy said.

"I'm not mad, Sammy boy, it was the best thing that could have happened. That was just a show and it just helped cement our story in his mind." I touched my index finger to my temple.

Sammy broke out into a world class grin "I think you are the clever one, Mr. Mark."

"Sammy, what did the numbers say was going to happen?"

"The numbers say good sir, and you say good." We both laughed a real laugh.

We were back at Best Western by 11am, we sat in silence waiting for the phone to ring.

"Do the numbers, Sammy". I was seeking a little relief from uncertainty myself.

"Okay, Mr. Mark, let's see what they say," he pulled out a fresh scrap of paper. It looked like a torn paper grocery bag, It wasn't until that I noticed he was using a pencil nub. How much time did he spend doing this? I wondered. But so far it had been accurate. "The numbers keep saying good, this whole thing, it all gon be good".

"What's a winner for you no can run past you," Sammy said.

We sat in silence for another hour. The phone rang, I answered on the fourth ring. It was indeed Nick.

"I'm sorry, I forget what you said when we first met. I have to admit I was a little carried away and that was rude of me. Come to dinner tonight and we will make a price and do business." "What do you say?" He took my silence as a confirmation.

"Oh and Mark, just you." Nick said.

"Why?"

"It's nothing. It's just that we don't need your partner for this negotiation, okay? Trust me."

I hung up and I looked at Sammy.

"Hey', I said. "I got bad news."

Sammy interrupted, "I know, I heard; that phone is loud. It's not bad news. I'll wait here". Sammy stretched out his legs and cracked a smile to let me know he wasn't offended.

"Thanks, Sammy."

The day went by quickly and by the time night fell the temperature had dropped to the high 30s. I got off the bed and took off the money belt, I counted out five thousand dollars and handed it to Sammy. I began to put on my boots and I grabbed a scarf out of my trench coat pocket before I put the leather trench coat on. I pulled my hair out from under my jacket and zipped up the inside lining. "I'll be back Sammy, but if I'm not, call this number on the desk. You ask for Eli and you tell him who you are and that something's gone wrong. You're technically paid, but if you help me out a little longer, there will be a little bonus for you when I get back."

Sammy nodded, "I was planning on staying as you put your boots on even without a bonus; I have to see how this turns out. Man this is *craze*" he used the Sierra Leonean Krio adaptation of the word crazy. "But the numbers are on your side, Mr. Mark, that is pure truth."

"From your lips to God's ears," I said. I won't deny, this had turned into a game for me. I wanted to accomplish big things, the band, for example, no one goes into the music business without contemplating that only one percent of all the people that try ever get to call it a career.

I felt that I had to accomplish this if I had any chance of accomplishing that, and not because of the money alone. The money could facilitate the time but not the talent or the desire. I am the one that would have to use the time that money provided wisely. I couldn't understand how it was that musicians who were serious had any time to be at the local rock bar, with all the other rock guys trying to be rockstars and everyone has the same story. I had already spent years as a traveling musician and I looked up to those guys when I was young, and I still respect what it takes but I needed to prove to myself that I could do, I don't know.... big things? All I knew is I had to do it, and to me there was a correlation with being successful in the music business.

I gave the cab driver the now familiar address of the exchange house. I entered the lobby and as I did so, the brown door outside of the cage that leads into the house buzzed. I grabbed it quickly and gave a wave of thank you at the camera. I could hear voices upstairs, my heart began beating a little faster, I hadn't considered that there might be other dinner guests. I heard the automatic locks of the downstairs door. I arrived on the first landing, which is to say the second floor—the floor the business offices were on. It was dimly lit, down at the end of the floor, his office light was on.

"Mr. Fareed?" I heard him say, "Come, come."

As I walked into his office, I saw he was sitting with a large pile of guilders on the desk and a beat up old leather duffel bag on the floor. I stepped in and said "Good evening Nick."

"Good evening to you." he responded. "So what's this we haven't agreed on a price yet?"

"Sure we have. You'll say 1.9, I'll say 1.5; you'll say 1.8 and I'll say 1.7, to which you will say yes. So why bother with the muck about?"

I took the stone out of my coat pocket and set it on the desk next to his pile of money. I unwrapped it with my left hand. It was quite an awesome sight. If only it were real. What difference did that make now, the 1.7 was frickin real and I hadn't even taken my coat off.

"The bag is complimentary. It's old and smells like goat but it will get you and the money back to the hotel." Nick said.

"I think it's very cool-looking actually, Nick" I said. I shouldn't have done that as he seemed to reconsider giving it to me, then just as quickly as the thought had come he shrugged it off and started loading the cash into the bag four and four bricks at a time. When there were just a few bricks left on the desk, he asked me to finish putting them into the duffel.

As I reached for the money, he took the stone off the desk.

"So this is 1.7 million US equivalent, I know you're a bank but I didn't get to count it." I said. "No, it's not." he said. I looked to see if he was kidding. "It's one million. They are counting the rest in the vault. It will be ready in just a few minutes." His expression was deadpan, like he was reading entries off a spreadsheet in a boring meeting, but his eyes glimmered like a hammerhead's. "Finish putting your money away, I have to show this to someone."

FUCK—GODDAMN IT—MOTHER FUCKING. I didn't say a word of that, I just thought it. There it was—the other shoe had just dropped. "Should you not finish with me before you fly off with the diamond?" I asked.

"It's in the vault; it's not ready. They would have called me. I'll pick it up on the way back. Relax, it's not leaving the house, the person who is going to look at it for me is here; he's a dinner guest tonight." Nick said. And he whisked off to go up the next flight of stairs toward the sound of the voices, which had gotten noticeably louder.

I had one million in the bag and I was in sight of the door. But it needed to be unlocked remotely or buzzed, as we say. Maybe I could kick it down and run. I thought but then—no, fuck!

He was off in the house with the diamond and he'd got a diamond guy, I was absolutely sure I was caught and I mean I was really scared. I couldn't even leave without the money. I had walked right into this trap like a total idiot. How did I wind up locked in without the diamond in my possession?

I heard him coming back down the stairs, and wondered if this was the moment of truth, but it wasn't. He didn't have the rest of the money either.

"Come on now, you have to stay for dinner—your money is here. Your jacket and your money can be left in my office. This place is a fortress," Nick said.

Fuckin' great. I was beginning to sweat and I took off the coat, I had no choice now. I began to wonder if I had some plausible deniability, maybe I could say I didn't know it was moissanite either. You know griffs are going sideways on you when you start planning your defense in your mental dialogue.

I walked upstairs determined to play it off no matter what, I began to regain my composure, I could remind him that he himself had tested it on his diamond detector and that I only had one year's experience.

The first room we walked into was very classy, expensive tile, covered in even more lavish Persian rugs, and dominated by a glass display case that stood 6 feet tall in the back of the room and eclipsed a whole wall. Inside tastefully illuminated by downlights were statues of stone, mostly of heads. Some looked to be quite ancient and it was said that they carried religious significance to the tribes in Sierra Leone—that they could even be ensouled.

I had forgotten to mention that I had been given one on the first trip with Shirley. The man on the beach had said to me, "You take this and you will see it's value and you will come back and you will pay me then. If you realize this value and you don't come back, it will bring you bad luck until you do."

I didn't believe it at the time but a few years later, I had an occurrence that made me change my mind. But that's another story.

There were a few guests in the room including the suited Scandinavians. I wondered if they would be the ones arresting me or if they would simply beat me to death. I'm playing it off now but believe me I was beyond petrified.

Nick introduced me again to the two large men, but I couldn't tell you their names. I remember I apologized for my behavior—it was out of an over abundance of caution. We walked into the next room where there was only one guest and he was sitting down and holding a guitar. It appeared he knew some barre chords. It took me a moment to realize it was Max.

"This is my partner Max Hasheem." He gestured towards Max "Nice to meet you," I said, as Max and I clasped hands as though we had never seen each other. I made small talk about the relics that were in this room too. Max was quite the bullshitter himself. He was giving a stellar performance pretending he didn't know me.

Once we had faked our way through the usual pleasantries, Nick said "Mark, one more room, come, come, meet my wife and girl." We ascended another flight of stairs and arrived at a large kitchen.

Again I didn't retain a single name. Nick offered me a drink by way of his wife but I declined and somehow she didn't understand me. For a moment, I thought I should just take her up on the drink and lose three years of sobriety. The temporary courage of alcohol was what I desperately needed. The clock was ticking and every second I was in that house separated from the stone, the pressure was growing, as was the danger and the risk of being found out. Somehow the words '*a drink is the last thing I need*' popped into my head. And I just used sign language to tell her no thank you. Nick had disappeared again. I left the kitchen and began to look for the room with Max. Navigating the house alone for the first time was confusing, but I knew we had walked up a flight of stairs to get to the kitchen. So I went down a flight. There appeared to be two staircases on each floor. I was starting to get it, I made my way back to the room where Max was and he was still there, only now he had a Scotch in hand.

"He has the diamond" I mouthed more than whispered. Max just gave one quick nod in acknowledgment."

"Are you the diamond guy?" I whispered.

"I don't think he's here yet" Max whispered back.

So that's where he kept running off to. He came back and Max switched the conversation back to voodoo heads without missing a beat. "Back on that, are you?" Nick said. "Mark, where's your drink?"

"He doesn't drink," Max answered, Nick cocked his head at Max for a second and Max just realized that neither of them had any way of knowing that. Realizing that he had just fucked up, Max recovered with, "He just told me." holding up his own drink. Which I followed with "Yes he just offered me one a moment or so ago."

Max began to wander out of the room casually as a few other guests reached the door. I approached Nick before he could get caught up in greeting the influx of new arrivals

"Nick we've got unfinished business."

"After dinner, after dinner." He kept insisting. The guests were moving towards the table now and I was caught in the general flow. I knew it was a great sign of disrespect but I had no choice so I went as far in the house as I could go, which was back down to the office floor and into his office where

I knew he would have to follow. I had to turn this around on him. "Look we have unfinished business, I don't want to disrespect you, but you bring me to a dinner where I am going to be very uncomfortable talking about what I do. And then we don't finish counting the money but the stone disappears. How do I know you are not trying to have it cleaved as we speak, and if it fails there would go my half of the money?" I asked.

"I've been upstairs for half an hour but I am not comfortable waiting any longer."

"You must at least come upstairs for one dessert, then you may go." He wasn't taking no for an answer, so I went back upstairs with him and sat down at the table. "I'm sorry you can't stay long." said a young woman's voice from behind a hijab as she placed a rolled pastry of some sort in front of me as well as a cup of strong smelling coffee or maybe tea. Max was sitting in conversation with one of the wives of one of the guests. But he did shoot me a couple of nervous glances. I ate about half my pastry and about that time, Nick left the table again. I thought this is it. But this time he came back looking frustrated and a little angry, but he wasn't looking at me, so it had to be the fact that his diamond expert was still not here. That was literally all I could take. It's strange but when things get really scary or I get really nervous things seem to go into slow motion.

But I stood up with the idea of making a bit of a scene about having to beg off the rest of the evening. "Excuse me, please, I haven't had the honor of speaking to most of you yet, however something has come up and I have to beg for my leave. Please forgive me and enjoy the rest of your evening." I departed from the table and made my way down the two flights of stairs to where the office was. I grabbed my coat and put it on then I took the bag with the money and I headed towards the stairs. Nick was coming down as I got to the door. At this point I was beginning to have the upper hand again. Where the hell was his fucking diamond guy anyway? I felt like I had endured just enough time to not keep taunting the gods, the expert was clearly late and that wasn't my fault. At this point the stone had been out of my hands for an hour, Nick was insisting that I return to dinner but I countered, "The only way out of this deal is to give me back the stone in the same condition I gave it to you, and that's why you pay cash." I held out the duffel bag at arm's length as though I were willing to push it into his hands if it would get me my mountain crystal back quicker. He recoiled not wanting to blow this deal or lose his chance to have the stone appraised by a third party.

"Where is the rest of my money or I'm going to begin to be a loud belligerent American. You saw me with the two gargantuans, so I know you don't doubt me." My words dripped with conviction and the unmistakable fullness of self-righteousness.

Whatever fear or doubt Nick had about the stone, it wasn't about what I had just hung my hat on, he wasn't worried about the tension problem at all but there was something just not quite right about the stone to him, and he would have been absolutely right. But the fact that I was only worried for the stone's well-being until fully paid at least relaxed any doubt he had about me. That was not the concern of a person trying to sell you a fake diamond.

"I'll have you buzzed out," Nick said. "What about the rest of my money"? I asked. "They will give it to you through the window" he said.

"Fine, Nick, it was a pleasure doing business with you, hopefully, next time will be smoother." And I headed down the stairs, man, I couldn't believe I was finally on the move after over an hour in there. The door buzzed and I was now standing out in the lobby with a million dollars. A million dollars was a hell of a lot of money in '91.

I could see the cab stand from where I was standing. Part of me just wanted to break and run for the cab, but leaving $700k behind might be a red flag. I knew they were watching. I could see the cameras but I never saw a camera room, which meant they were in a room I hadn't entered. Time felt like it was dragging by and for another 10 minutes, I ground my teeth sitting there. But now I felt that I had again waited the right amount of time to start losing it. I paced to the door and back. At one point I dropped the million dollars to the floor, just for effect, I pointed at my watch and gesticulated at the camera. I was at a breaking point. Fuck it, let 'em chase me. Just as I was deciding that I was going to bolt, the inside of the cage door buzzed and opened, there were two youngish Arab looking gentlemen with a milk crate-sized box full of currency. Somehow I didn't break and run. I shifted my weight off the balls of my feet and strolled up to the cage. The currency was coming through the window slot and I went as fast as I could without looking panicked. The bag filled up and there was still like 70 grand on the counter, I put some in each boot, as much as would fit in my coat's inside pocket, and a couple of bricks in the outside pockets. Just the heft of the bag was exciting and scary at the same time. I was taking off with a lot of their money. I walked to the double doors and turned to face back inside, naturally I gave an exaggerated bow to the camera. I'll never forget focusing on my boots as I walked as calmly as I could, still resisting the urge to run, the heavy leather trench coat now heavier with money. I finally reached a cab and asked for the Best Western on Hoofstraat. As we pulled away, I turned and looked out of the back window of my cab, just in time to see another cab stop at the double doors, and watch a gentleman exit. If that was the diamond expert, I think I had a 15-minute jump on them. My bags were packed in the room. I went up to grab it and there was Sammy. Out of the 70 grand or so in my jacket, I gave Sammy a $50k bonus. "Sammy, I never lost faith in the numbers. Now take this and run for it. You're on your own."

Sammy gave me a hug that almost crippled me, and he said, "I shall never forget you. You are my first good fortune." I said "Ditto, Sammy."

"What does this mean 'ditto'?" he asked,

"It's what you say when you want to say the same thing back... man, they're going to probably be here in ten minutes. And Max maybe sooner. Later days, my friend".

I stopped at the front desk and checked out. I got my passport back and I paid the clerk 100 guilders to tell anyone who called or asked that I was still checked in. He said he would and I peeled off another fifty to be sure. I made it back into a cab in what felt like record time. There was no sign of Max yet either. I had the driver take me to Leidseplein Square. Overlooking the square there is a Marriott hotel, I decided to stay the night there. I asked for and got the penthouse suite.

I went to the payphone in the lobby before I went up to my room and called Best Western to ask if there were any calls. The clerk said the phone hadn't stopped ringing, and I'd had a few visitors but that he would be there all night. I booked multiple flights out of the country on the off chance that my adversaries had a way of looking into such things. Satisfied that I was relatively undetectable, I went up to my room and I walked in and closed the door. I took the money out of the smelly leather case and out of my coat and I spread it out on the bed. I noticed the mini bar and for the second time that day, I thought of a drink and then thought better of it. Instead, I threw open the drapes and gazed down at stacks of guilders about a foot high neatly arranged on satin sheets flanked by the ancient Amsterdam cityscape buzzing with life and activity below. If there was an inner Renaissance Master painter in me, that image is what he would draw. I had adversaries looking for me down there and the exhilaration of victory was coursing through my veins. Who knew how far they would pursue me to avenge this loss?

What had begun as an epiphany delivered via stolen cable had manifested into a fortune via a stolen stone that would see me performing in front of tens of thousands of people, exploring the cutting-edge of science in at least one tale for a later time, and continuing to apprehend the magic of music to this very day. There are still a thousand mysteries awaiting an intrepid explorer in this world, several I'm sure in the beautiful continent of Africa. But that's crazy thinking right? To imagine that your fortune awaits out there perhaps in the discovery of the lost sarcophagus of Alexander The Great hijacked by king Ptolemy - it's rumored that its still interred somewhere in Egypt though perhaps submerged -amidst alluvial diamonds in the shifting sands, or to discover the science of the mysterious roots long applied but poorly understood by the the healers that despite their divinations have not yet discovered that what is true of their knowledge could make them kings in the west properly applied. I mean if it were that easy everyone would be doing it.

THE END

The authors Mark Christian (center) Troy Christian (right) and design specialist Tyler Christian (left)